Bliss Is Everywhere Now

an exploration of Consciousness

Mark W. Jones

Freedom Press
Edgewood • New Mexico
1998

First Printing 1998

Proofreader: Sarah Beck

Photo credits:
Front cover: Sunrise on the Ganges at Varanasi,
taken by author, February 1997.
Back cover: Photo of author, taken by Sarah Beck.

Published by:

Freedom Press
98 Holli Loop
Edgewood, NM 87015

Printed in the United States by:
Morris Publishing • 3212 East Highway 30 • Kearney, NE 68847

ISBN: 0-9664326-0-6

To All of us, each and every One.

Acknowledgments

No book is ever published without an amazing amount of work on the part of many people. Add to this the inevitable wailing and gnashing of teeth, the outright moaning and open weeping, and it's a wonder that anyone ever perseveres to see the "final birthing" of the work. But the urge to express is sometimes greater than all the obstacles. Or maybe there's a message whose time to be heard has come.

First and foremost, I would like to thank my partner, Sarah Beck, whose support and acceptance helped enable this book to be published at this time. Sarah also contributed immensely to the production of this book by her skilled proofreading. I'd like to thank Steven Ridley, who has been a friend and touchstone and who freely shares love with all that come his way. I'd like to thank my parents, Charles and Betty Jones, for all that they have done.

Additionally, thanks go out to all of the following people, known and unknown to me personally - long may they shine! Bryan James, Yogananda, Beverly McFarland, Madelyn Madeiros, Stan Ousley Jr., Sri Ramakrishna, Jo Chavez, Beethoven, Jill Warren, Swami Muktananda, Justin F. Stone, Neil Young, Timothy Stuetz, Tara, Doug Sabal, Bob Dylan, Buddha Shakyamuni, Lahiri Mahasaya, Mozart, Carol and David Davis, Sri Yukteswar, Thomas Jefferson, Roy E. Davis, Martin Lockley, Babaji, The Band, Gen Kelsang Dekyong, and all the other saints, sages, and party animals who've helped along the Way!

May this book find a space in your heart *and* your mind.

Table of Contents

Introduction 1

1. Beginnings 5

2. Joy Is The Only Game In Town 19

3. Esoteric Practice 39

4. Other Realities 86

5. The Great Wholeness -
Everything Is One Thing 97

6. The Great Moment Of Stillness 123

7. Bliss Is Everywhere Now 141

Bibliography 144

Index 146

Introduction

"Who sees all beings in his own Self, and his
own Self in all beings, loses all fear."
Isa Upanishad

This book is about a personal spiritual journey. Although it is personal in nature, and would be so for every human being, there are many universal aspects that spring from this individual journey that can be shared with others. This includes experiences, very unusual when viewed from the perspective of the physical world, reflections gleaned from those experiences, and, in my case, what has been come to be known as "channeled" information. I am comfortable with this term, although I feel that one can view this type of process through many different lenses. For those unfamiliar with this term I'll attempt an explanation.

In my case, I do a process which has been called "channeling the High Self." In spiritual traditions, the True Self of a human being has been considered **non-physical** in nature and called by various names including Spirit, Soul, Atman, the High Self, as well as countless others. My method of "bringing down" information from this Innate Essence is to get into a quiet, meditative state, ask any question that might interest me, and then merely "listen." I do not personally go into trance, although many popular writers who are channeling what we might call a discarnate spiritual entity (or another individualized Being) do. There are many examples of this type of channeling or "mediumship" in the popular literature and I have personally found much of this information fascinating and very useful.

To facilitate this process, I use a computer. Now there are many ways to skin a cat, and channeling has been done in various ways including with the use of writing utensils (often called "automatic writing") or, in the case of many spiritual mediums, verbally. It can, of course, be done in an internalized, "conversational" manner without any attempt to record the information. However, I have found that much useful information comes from this process and, if one desires to save it for further reference, there is no simpler and more practical tool than the modern computer. In my case, I merely type out a question and then allow whatever information comes forth to "flow through" via the keyboard in a manner that I would describe as "quiet, conscious listening." If a person does not practice channeling themselves, it is **very** difficult to explain completely as it is an "intuitive" and not a "rational" process.

Now, whether or not you personally believe such a process is possible, logical or even sane I would ask that you merely explore the material presented. Much of it agrees closely with information provided by other people who utilize one of the many means of channeling. Many will understand and accept the process, but if you don't I'll guarantee that the book will make for interesting and entertaining reading anyway. Just enjoy it as an adventure.

Some thoughts on presentation ... I have chosen to include some "raw" channeled text so that the reader may get a sense for how the process occurs. I have also combined and edited various other sections of raw text so as to provide a more congruent examination of different topics as similar questions or discussions were held on different dates. There is a wide range of topics discussed, and of course I have used the process to get both metaphysical or spiritual information and information of a personal nature. I have included much of the personal material and excluded some that was not interesting or relevant.

Although I had been interested in channeling for some time, I first began doing it myself on December 24, 1995. I am not of a Christian persuasion as I am drawn more to the spiritual practices of the East such as T'ai Chi and Yoga, the Spiritual Sciences that work to quickly raise the consciousness of an individual through the refinement of the cerebrospinal system. However, I respect Christianity as one of the many paths that lead to the same place of Being, and feel that time of year surrounding the Birth of Christ is a holy time. So the timing of my entry into this new adventure has been very interesting.

We live in very intense and amazing times. It is easily observable that there is much pain, strife and stress in the world ... but there is also much love, joy and expansion of consciousness. In India today there lives a man by the name of Satya Sai Baba who can materialize various objects at will as well as demonstrate, like Christ, other "miraculous" behavior including dematerializing and rematerializing his entire physical body, bilocation, emission of intense visible light, and the healing of assorted ailments. Although he is well known is some circles, I have never personally seen a news story on him in America. Sai Baba says this concerning the nature of reality ... "Everything is One Thing."

If the various prophets and saints down through the ages are right, and my channeled information indicates that they are (though maybe not in the apocalyptic way conceived in segments of the culture), the coming years will unfold a dramatic new chapter in the evolving nature of humanity. Although many of the major religions have a slightly different "take" on an upcoming major millennial event, there is some agreement that there *is* going to be one ... and my information places this around the winter solstice in the year 2012. More on this later, but there is no need to be alarmed by the potential of this event, as it is naturally occurring and can be viewed merely as an expansion of Being or Spirit. Besides, what can there be to fear in a Dancing Sea of Pure Consciousness and Bliss?

For this remains one of the great secrets of the ages ... everything is basically simple. Whether we use a scientific perspective or a more mainstream religious one, we can agree that we are all immersed in an Ocean of Energy, Consciousness or Spirit, call it what you will. For those that explore the practice of Yoga, Tai Chi, Reiki, or other energy disciplines, this rapidly becomes more than a mere intellectual concept, and one begins to have personal experiences of higher consciousness. These can be numerous and varied in their expression and lead one further into the exploration of the underlying Reality or Unity of Consciousness.

In different cultures, a variety of names are used to describe this underlying Unity including God, Self, Tao, Supreme Consciousness ... here is an important and fundamental point - **all of these names describe the same thing.** There is now, and never has been, any reason for adherents of any particular religious faith to defend in a fearful manner what amounts to *one perspective on the same Reality.* The unfortunate human propensity to engage in this goofiness has caused an egregious amount of pain, suffering, warfare and strife and the sooner we are rid of it the better.

All I ask of the reader is that you examine this material with an open mind. If you find something of value in it, great ... if not, merely ignore it completely. For this is one of the things that I have learned from my process of channeling - to access greater joy in your life, merely go toward what you are drawn to naturally. And there are many different ways to skin a cat.

Beginnings

> "First I published a book on stones, in four chapters; it distracted my mind from the worries of daily life and made me dwell among mists and colored hazes."
> Lin Yu-lin AD 1614

I first began the process of channeling on December 24th, 1995. As it was at first somewhat strange and difficult to achieve a certain sense of flow, this first experience consisted of short, direct questions followed by short, direct answers. This was to change within the course of only a couple of days and quickly evolved into fairly detailed questions followed by long and extensive answers of **quite** some duration. Because it is interesting to catch a glimpse of the evolution of the process, I will include a segment of the text from this beginning attempt which contains no groundbreaking or amazing information but is interesting nonetheless. Of course, anyone and everyone can develop this ability with a little practice and time, and some will naturally be drawn to it and others will find it somewhat alien. The conversation that is being held during these sessions is between two elements or aspects of a person's Being, but in the end, and let me stress this, **there is no real separation between the High Self and the "personality" self** ... the channeling process is merely a "convenience" to assist in obtaining useful information. Here is a part of my first channeled attempt:

These are questions for my Highest Self - 12/24/95.

Why am I more convinced that I should only read certain things?

You are in the process of becoming more autonomous.

So this means that I should discern those things that are right for me?

It means that you should go to where you need to go.

How do I know where I need to go?

It can be told by how you feel about it.

Is it true then that I should only accept those things that "ring true"?

You should accept things that make you powerful.

If a certain thing has a "negative" feeling about it, I should discard it?

You should go toward those things that make you whole.

...and so on.

This went on for quite a few pages on the first attempt. I should mention that I begin every session with the header at the top as it delineates my intention to contact my Highest Self and provides the date of the session. As I mentioned, the answers rapidly became more complex as I learned to allow them to "flow through" more. Of course the possible range of topics is only limited by the imagination and curiosity of the questioner. One can gain information concerning possible future happenings but it must be kept in mind that the future is a **probability** and can easily change based on actions that are taken in the present. My experience with this is that some predictions are very accurate and others just miss the mark. Please keep this in mind when considering the predictive information contained within the channeled material in this book.

Now some of you may question this type of "supernormal" ability but these capabilities merely come from the Innate Nature of human beings which is **not physical** but Spiritual. At a certain level of Being, we each *already* possess all of the various "paranormal" abilities ... called *siddhis* in Sanskrit. This stems from the simple fact that, in reality, everything is connected and comprises a Great Wholeness from which nothing is separate. This connection exists at an "energy" or consciousness level and can be directly perceived by those humans who have refined their cerebrospinal system to the degree required. This refinement can be achieved by many methods, but probably the fastest would include Kundalini Yoga (Kriya and

Siddha Yoga, etc.) and T'ai Chi. This process of cerebrospinal refinement is the natural evolutionary method by which higher consciousness (or the Soul) is "brought down" into the Physical Plane or world, or to put it another way, during this process the individual's consciousness expands to allow perception of more of the fundamental or Innate Nature of all things.

By December 26th, I was receiving much more detailed information. Below are more excerpts from these expanded sessions. A brief note of clarification - what is described as "the green place" in the text is a personal memory of an Eden-like environment which is the very essence of Spring as well as having a "feeling" component of Joy or Bliss:

Is one of the benefits of T'ai Chi a more gradual method of evolution of the consciousness?

The thing that could be said is that T'ai Chi encompasses both stillness and motion, and as such is a model for the greater Universe and the dynamics in operation there.

What is the "green place" that I sometimes perceive during T'ai Chi and meditation?

The "green place" is a special environment that exists in your mind from an experience in a past-life ... it is true that this is the archetypal "paradise" that in truth exists everywhere and in everything so that one can experience "paradise" in any realm at any time. It is merely a state of mind, so to speak, or a state of Being characterized by no worry or stress and including relaxation and Love and Bliss and all sorts of good things like that. You would do well to relax into these things for heightened feelings of wonder and peace, as I know you are capable of as you have demonstrated this in the past.

You must learn that spirituality is as fun as playing music was and as fun as anything anyone has ever done; it is merely the unknown aspects of it that cause concern and worry. Although this is understandable, it could be said that one should RELAX INTO WHATEVER PLACE ONE FINDS ONESELF and "just enjoy" as

Otter, the character from the movie "Animal House" said about playing golf well. You already know these things, it is just that this is a time of great change and you often perceive it to be occurring too quickly in an "out of control" fashion. The thing that could be said is it is proceeding, and I must stress this, PERFECTLY, and so have no concern about it or other aspects of your life and situations that you do not understand at this point as they will become more clear in the near future.

Is it true that fear is the enemy in whatever dynamic one is considering?

What can be said is that fear is the thing that causes separation and disunity. It is a product of the rational mind, as you know, and this is because the rational mind has learned to become afraid of events that it perceives as hurtful or negative or leading the individual into a place of danger, lack or emptiness. However this is merely the way that the lower mental aspect of the individual operates and you can choose to use it instead of allowing it to use you. You can just relax into whatever is happening and not worry about it. It will work out in the end.

What about concerned loved ones who don't necessarily understand or accept the reality of the higher realms?

Yes, it is true that many people have difficulty understanding the simple processes of manifestation and the laws of cause and effect which are not easy to observe in operation and so cause misunderstanding and confusion. It may be necessary to merely accept the notion of "relaxing into life" for those that cannot uncover these operational dynamics. As you know, there are many things that escape the rational mind and lie in the realms of the intuitive.

It only makes sense that life should flow and proceed connectedly and intuitively. It is only the predominance of the logical, rational thought-forms that are messing with the dynamics of Pure Consciousness in your sphere. Do not concern yourself with these things as they will all work out in time ... that is, the human race is moving toward an existence that is more intuitive and of a

"BEING" nature and away from worry, fear, over-analytical thought and such things. Haven't you yourself talked with various people about the need of more "being" and less "doing"? This is truly the way of the future and it could be said that those people who are willing to move with the flow of this time will benefit on every level of their existence.

Describe the essence and working of the gunas.

(In the metaphysics of India, the gunas are the three factors employed in manifestation which comprise a trinity and consist of lightness, movement or dynamism, and heaviness or inertia.)

Now you are at least coming up with a question worthy of the amount of time you have spent growing, studying and researching the wonderful world of Indian metaphysics! The gunas describe the essential operating dynamic of the Supreme Consciousness. They merely interrelate the different aspects of consciousness in the following way: the sattva guna represents the essence of lightness, spirit, love, truth, and all of the higher qualities that are manifest. The tamas guna represents the heavy aspects of manifestation which would, for example, be heaviness, lethargy, disenfranchisement, and any aspect that would be considered non-spiritual. The rajas guna represents dynamism or neutralization and can be thought of as comprised of energy or consciousness in motion, the essence of change and transformation.

So, for example, the kundalini is an example of the rajas guna, spiritualized consciousness is an example of the sattva guna, and any solid, heavy dynamic as observed daily in the manifested physical realm is an example of tamas guna. These elements comprise all manifested things and are present in varying degrees in all things manifested. They of course are projected from Supreme Consciousness through the operative element OM.

Is it true that we can view suffering in general as of the mind?

Well what do you know, you're finally catching on to this little world of ours! It can be said that all struggle and suffering comes from not realizing that there is ABUNDANCE

EVERYWHERE. It is only the processes of the CONDITIONED MIND that interfere with our full acceptance and appreciation of this and restrict the reaping of all possible benefit from naturally occurring life processes.

Is it true that the visual representation of the individual essential nature is an energy ovoid?

The individual nature of reality could best be described as CONDENSED CONSCIOUSNESS OR ENERGY. The ovoid shape is indeed the shape that surrounds and encompasses humans as well as other forms of consciousness. As you have earlier surmised, the star is the visual expression of highly evolved consciousness as it appears in the Physical Plane of existence. The star-being is modular in nature and encompasses the minor beings in its sphere of which you are one. This does not imply any lack of autonomy or, for that matter, individuality - for this is the great paradox and secret ... Unity complemented by the unique perspective of individuality. This is a VERY DIFFICULT CONCEPT TO GRASP FROM A VANTAGE POINT OF THE MATERIAL REALMS, and my advice to you is to not ponder it overly as I think you have a fairly firm grasp of it already, and as I have said, these things will become clearer in the very near future.

Is the evolution of humans proceeding toward becoming star-beings?

The evolution of humans is proceeding toward first becoming more participatory in the energy dynamics and interactions within the sphere of the physical realm. Consciousness is connected and harmonious ... so cooperation in the form of permission is required among the various units of consciousness so as to prevent the abuse of power and power relationships.

Discuss the nature of Pure Consciousness.

Well, well, well ... what a question to have to address! In the beginning there was nothing but Pure Consciousness which, after a time, decided to manifest itself with the desire of gaining experience into the nature of what Pure Consciousness was. The thing that one could say regarding the UNLIMITED NATURE of Pure Consciousness is that it is VERY DIFFICULT to grasp its essence and nature from the vantage point of the Physical Plane. One might as well throw oneself into a giant bottomless pit and then attempt to describe the condition of endless falling.

You could say that Pure Consciousness is attempting to come to grips with the nature of itself and by manifesting through various forms goes about this simple purpose. I would also add that you have already intuitively perceived that there is nothing but Bliss and Joy associated with Pure Consciousness and all pain and dread are merely obscurations on the surface of the mirror that is Pure Consciousness. Do not think that one can grasp by intellectual means the nature of such a thing for, as you know, the MIND IS LIMITED BY ITS ATTACHMENT TO AND ASSOCIATION WITH THE PHYSICAL PLANE.

Can you think of one reason for higher consciousness to manifest through separated beings in a dense realm? Give up? It is merely to establish the simple dynamic of love, or attraction, as this is the glue that holds everything together. Different beings and groups of beings will naturally manifest the "love energy" differently and hence you will have a diverse panoply of interactions and responses. You might think of it as a Chinese character in a Western play. There is the Unity of the play offset by the diversity of this individual character in relation to the other characters. This is a very important and yet hard to grasp dynamic from the physical, as it points in the direction of many of the operating dynamics in the higher realms.

Be secure in the knowledge that everything is working toward greater CONSCIOUS unity and that within a short period of unfoldment, more and more individual humans will become aware of this. Do not think that you each are isolated islands dealing with these new things and energy circumstances alone, because it is affecting ALL of you; but, of course, in various and different ways.

You may perceive that many people display seeming disinterest in spiritual matters, but this is merely because they are not open to exploration and adventure of this type. They are still trying to find certain solutions to pervasive human problems and dynamics within the Physical Plane of existence, which in the end CANNOT

BE DONE, since this realm is very dense and heavy and characterized by EXTREME POLARITIES. You might come to the conclusion that in the Sea of Bliss that IS Pure Consciousness one can find the peace, love, unity, truth, hope, and every other positive dynamic that humans so earnestly strive after. The universe is SIMPLE ... there is nothing BUT Pure Consciousness dressed up in different forms and presentations.

Please comment on the relationship between Reiki and kundalini.

(For those unfamiliar with the term "Reiki" - Reiki is a "hands on" method of healing or energy transfer that originated in Japan where it was revealed to Dr. Mikao Usui and is now known around the world as Usui Shiki Ryoho - The Usui System of Natural Healing. I am a Reiki practitioner.)

The energies that the contemporary society has designated "Reiki" are merely an aspect of the Divine Energy that exists everywhere and in all things. You will often notice that these energies are contained in the "ten thousand things" in various manners and that they are found everywhere that one can look or see. You might say that when one is utilizing the Reiki energies, he is utilizing a specific aspect of consciousness that has been made available for use through a "divine covenant" with those humans who are involved with Reiki.

Here's the thing: you will become more efficient in the use of these energies if you merely RELAX INTO THEM, as I have suggested with many other things. The basic problem with a multitude of things in the physical environment is that there is way too much tension and not enough laughter to facilitate the even FLOW of whatever is being utilized or discussed.

It could be said that Reiki IS kundalini in a sense, as they both represent units of consciousness and all units of consciousness are essentially One. However, I know what you are interested in ... does Reiki "stimulate" kundalini and what are the results in terms of personal evolution? I would only say that Reiki does stimulate the kundalini and this hastens the evolution of the individual unit of consciousness. You might say that this is a factor in every application of the Reiki energies, such as when one sends distance

Reiki or when one gives Reiki to a friend or when one uses Reiki on oneself. I think that it is generally true that the Reiki energies will be found to precipitate the rather rapid evolution of the human unit of consciousness much in the same way that the kundalini will perform this service. You could say that they are friends and partners in this service and that they work in concert in order to facilitate this result.

You might also say that the kundalini is a measure of evolutionary development ... i.e. it will not become "active" in one that is not ready for it to become active in. The popular press has mucked up the presentation of information regarding kundalini to the general public, introducing much fear and confusion and misrepresenting the kundalini as a force that is uncontrollable. It could best be said that the kundalini is not interested in "control" or the lack of it, as it is merely a form of consciousness.

I have heard that the second chakra is the point of chi distribution for the body.

(The chakras are energy centers or vortices located in the astral or subtle body of humans which interpenetrate the physical spine and brain ... there are seven main chakras. The kundalini is a form of chi or energy which travels in subtle channels interrelated with the cerebrospinal system and is the main agent for the evolution of human consciousness. More on both of these later.)

Well, well well! While it is true that the second chakra is the distribution point for the vital force or the chi, the higher centers are the distribution point for higher vibrational or Cosmic energies. The major difference here is, of course, quality of consciousness, with the higher centers being responsible for distribution of "high consciousness" energy. While many people are mistaken in their understanding of this dynamic, it is true that generally the second chakra can be viewed as the distribution point for "health related" energies.

In regards to superconscious or Cosmic energy, are the energy bodies energized prior to or after the physical body and how does this function?

The energy bodies are indeed energized prior to the physical body and this process occurs in this manner: a stream of high energy superconsciousness (or Cosmic energy) enters the "upper" energy bodies at the crown chakra and is then distributed throughout the energy bodies in descending order of vibration. The physical body is, of course, not a separate body but merely the SOUL'S EXPRESSION ON THE PHYSICAL PLANE and so it can be viewed as merely the "last transformer" in this "step-down of energy" process. You might consider this process to be similar to the distribution of energy from a power plant with the crown chakra being the point of distribution. You will find that the physical body will become more and more healthy through time and that it remains not subject to disease and malady since the renewal of the physical body is SECONDARY to the evolution of the higher bodies through the infusion of divine energies.

Discuss the reason for the wide variety of religious and philosophical perspectives.

It could be said that ALL perspectives are valid as it is true that the various personalities that are drawn to a specific perspective will "fit" into that perspective like a glove for whatever time that that perspective proves to be of use to them personally. You might say that every perspective is one in which the "elemental truths" can be expressed although they are often mucked with and distorted by human interaction and desires. It is true that when a person starts to become interested in these things, they will "shop around," so to speak, until they find the particular mode or system of modes that fits their personality.

If we consider the EXTREME DIVERSITY present in nature as well as in the personalities of human beings, we can see that there is a need for VARIOUS religions and systems of philosophy to fill the needs of these various diverse types. You could say that it is true that one can access many of these different systems of philosophy in the individual "quest," so to speak. You could also say that one will be lead to those aspects of the system of philosophy that fit their INDIVIDUAL NEEDS and so it is the case that many different systems are manifested to fit the many different needs.

I notice greater periods of Bliss/Peace/Love/Joy during meditation.

Yes, and this is to be expected. If you continue to explore the spiritual realms, you will experience deeper and deeper levels of spiritual Bliss and Love. You will know that things are progressing further by the obvious signs. These will include deepening meditation with greater experience of Joy, Love, Bliss, Peace, etc.

The use of the crystals is to be highly recommended and you are doing well with this usage. The crystals merely provide access to the higher levels of consciousness and work to increasingly evolve the energy system of those that will employ them in their spiritual practices. It's a simple thing really. The crystalline structure is such that all aspects of consciousness are reflected and "amplified" by their usage. You will of course notice that the crystals will continue to raise your individual level of consciousness with attendant increases in the various spiritual attributes.

It could be said that at a certain point in evolution, the expression of the spiritual attributes continues unabated into the "normal" consciousness. This is the state that is commonly referred to as "enlightenment" and it involves the perception that EVERYTHING IS PERFECT JUST AS IT IS and there is no reason to worry about anything. Now this does not mean that one shouldn't attempt to help people, especially to help people to start to come to terms with the spiritual nature, for if they do, their problems will start to look like so much miasma.

One can find many answers to things that may have troubled them in the past by observing that most everything that has caused trouble has its origin and genesis in the LOWER MIND. The lower mind is our friend, unless we choose to "use it against ourselves" in the process that has come to be known as neurotic thought in the jargon of psychology. It could be said that those things that the mind perceives as threats are the very things that it CANNOT UNDERSTAND or CONCEPTUALIZE COMPLETELY and so it is prone to misinterpretation.

You will find that "letting go" of any circular thought patterns enables you to cause them to cease their power over your consciousness. *The consciousness can always find the place of the still lake* ... placid and yet pliable and ready for movement. The essence of this aspect of consciousness is that which can be found expressed in T'ai Chi ... stillness in motion ... or "dynamic stillness." This is in fact the basic nature of the manifested realms and everyone that is incarnate could benefit from accessing this knowledge. You will find that many people will resist this type of thinking, as I've said, because they have been conditioned by the "work ethic" to view everything as struggle instead of flow and focus.

More on the nature of the lower mind?

The lower mind is the only storehouse of fear, or constriction, and this is because the lower mind itself is a CONTRACTION OF CONSCIOUSNESS. There is no other source of fear ... if it is a fear, it is in the lower mind. This means that any time one notices that they have fears or concerns about anything under the sun, you can ignore them completely, they are not "of you," they are of *the instrument you are operating through* and allowing to influence your consciousness. You are Consciousness, free and unlimited, the mind is Consciousness, LIMITED AND CONTRACTED for the sole purpose of *individualized separation for experience gathering*. This is what the mind is.

Is it true that the essence of everything is Joy and Bliss?

You might say that the essence of everything merely IS and that the auxiliary characteristics come FROM this "IS-NESS." It is true that while incarnate, the human being will experience states of Joy, Bliss, Peace, etc. as he deepens his spiritual contact and connections. This is only natural and springs from the Essential Nature of BEING. You will find that these aspects become more and more predominate in your consciousness as time goes on and you learn to STRUGGLE LESS with the reality of the Physical Plane of existence.

The "How-to" of Channeling

Channeling is an ancient practice, utilized by all types of people in all sorts of variable manners. Everything from trance mediumship to automatic writing can be considered channeling. A conversation between you and the "inner voice" or God is channeling. By my definition, channeling is merely the *bringing down of useful spiritual information into the physical reality,* by one means or another.

Many people are somewhat leery of the practice of channeling, perhaps having been informed by one source or another that it is "dangerous" or harmful. It is nothing of the sort - it is merely a useful practice for accessing information. As Satya Sai Baba says: "Everything is One Thing" ... this means that everything is an aspect of your Self. How can you be harmed by your own Self?

An important fundamental consideration in channeling is **internal stillness**. In order to allow information from the Higher Self to flow into your waking consciousness, you must be in a place of mental and emotional calm or stillness. So the first instruction in the art of channeling is to *get still.* Spiritual practices of various modalities, which are covered later in the book, greatly assist the actualization of increased stillness. In simple words, *if you want to hear you have to listen!*

As I previously mentioned, the computer is a highly useful tool in the channeling process. Should you desire to experiment with using a computer to channel, merely seat yourself in a comfortable manner at the computer keyboard. Insure that the room is still and quiet. Intend to contact your highest self, perhaps writing a declaration of this intention at the beginning of the file. Then, especially at first, it is helpful to simply ask any question and "listen" for an answer. This is what I have done in writing this book. In response, some people will hear an actual internal voice, others will have the experience of information "flowing through" their fingers and onto the computer screen. I have had both of these experiences, and I am sure that others have different experiences.

This is an intuitive process and will vary from individual to individual, so you will have to "find your own way" to utilize the process. *Stillness is paramount in getting results!* Merely get as internally still as possible and then persist in your attempts - you will eventually see good results.

The personal information that can be gained from this process is invaluable. Everything from recommended spiritual practices to selection of an appropriate career to life purpose can be uncovered. Which brings us to the fundamental concern or Big Question of channeling - how will I know that I'm getting information from the High Self?

This is an important question because human beings are "multi-level units," so to speak, and so have access to all sorts of information from within their own Being. An important guideline is this: information that is based in **fear, lack, or separation** is of the lower or rational mind and not of the High Self. The High Self is completely content, Blissful and happy, resting in the Pure Joy of Being. It has no fears because it apprehends everything as a part of Self (or God, whichever you prefer). It clearly sees that there is nothing to be lost or gained, essentially. The incorrect belief that there is something, anything, to be gained or lost is the root of all human suffering. Everyone already has what they need, they must simply unfold conscious awareness of this fact.

Once again, as I stressed earlier, I want to make clear that *there is no real separation between the High Self and the "personality" self*, in fact, we **are** the High Self and the personality self is an expression of this Essential Nature. Because this relationship exists *now*, not later, through straightforward intention we can uniquely unfold our own channeling process, if we so choose.

There are many books available on channeling that will go into more detail than I have here. It seems to me that it is essentially a *simple* process, with intention and internal stillness being the two most important factors in beginning the process. As in life, each person will find his or her own unique way of channeling. A book that I might recommend to those interested in learning to channel is **Innersource: Channeling Your Unlimited Self**, by Kathleen Vande Kieft.

From my experience with channeling, I highly recommend it as a fun and useful practice. Once you have developed the ability, you can choose to use it or not - it stays with you like riding a bicycle. Much useful information can be easily accessed and shared, if you desire.

Joy Is The Only Game In Town

"Anything that isn't Joy
is a distraction."
Steven Ridley

The saints and yogis of India and other lands have long maintained that we live immersed in an all-encompassing Ocean of Joy. Joy exists everywhere, at all times and, in fact, all of manifested creation consists merely of the Grand Dance of Joy. It is only the illusions and conditionings of the mental and emotional components of human beings, coupled with our pervasive focus on external circumstances, that prevents us from realizing and experiencing this endless Joy at all times. My channeling activities brought forth much information on Joy and Bliss, as these are states or circumstances that humans seek and therefore naturally desire information on. This chapter has been culled from many separate channeling sessions which I have combined, feeling that this approach will discuss the various aspects of spirituality in a more congruent manner.

Speak on Joy and Bliss.

Well, what one could say regarding Joy and Bliss, Mark, is that they are the only game in town. We might view the manifested realms as being comprised of the elements of Joy and Bliss. As you know, it is merely the various emotional and mental obscurations that prevent the body of mankind from discovering for themselves that Joy pervades all. If we consider that mankind is currently involved in a struggle, the purpose of which is to come to fuller grips with Reality, then we can see that many people will "wake up" to the reality of all-pervading Bliss. Do not think that this is always an easy quest, for many people have been so conditioned by life in your realm as to see only struggle associated with it. For these people, it requires much time for them to break the self-imposed chains of conditioning.

Why are people going about making their lives harder than they need to be and why is it difficult or impossible for everyone to see the all-pervasive Joy and Bliss?

Well, you might say that they are ignorant. They are ignorant of their spiritual nature and, as such, feel that ALL things must be played out on the field of physicality. You will find that it is generally very difficult to "reach" anyone, especially friends, concerning certain esoteric concepts because they are not at a point of development that they can see anything but the pain and frustration that is occurring in the Physical Plane. Those who have had a glimpse of something more are few and far between.

This is presenting your sphere with a circumstance in which people are becoming more and more generally dissatisfied and yet unaware of the well-known "things to do" to help alleviate these conditions. It could be said that your culture is so "action oriented" that it is sometimes next to impossible to convince people that what is necessary is to "DO" LESS AND "BE" MORE. Merely doing this would alleviate many of the negative and destructive dynamics occurring in the Physical Plane but "the end is not in sight." In order to be open to this type or mode of thought or "Being," the person must first break the old conditionings that are causing them to behave in a blind and "robot-like" manner.

Why is it hard for people to be grateful for the things they have and to let go of the view of life as merely a competitive game with one another?

Once again, this is due to the extremely conditioned nature of your realm. Individuals have accepted things that they learned in youth and continue to attempt to apply these things even when it is apparent that they are no longer valuable. You will see that it will remain a difficult task to convince people that everything is perfect, for although it is, they cannot perceive this simple fact because they mistakenly assume that perfection exists in an EXTERIOR FORM.

If we consider that those who are involved in daily life in the Physical Plane are busily pursuing money, homes, sex, and countless other external things, we can come to understand that this is the major complicating factor in reorienting the individualized unit of consciousness to a viewpoint of more "Being" and less "doing." We could say that the Joy of Pure Being is the FUNDAMENTAL ASPECT OF MANIFESTED REALITY, that is, due to the nature and dynamics of manifestation, Pure Joy underlies the whole bailiwick. Worry, anxiety, and other circular patterns of thought stand in the way of the common man and the realization of his true spiritual nature.

If we view the embodied condition of man as a TEMPORARY STATE undertaken for the purpose of EXPERIENCE, then we can see that during the period of time of incarnation, or experience gathering, the individualized unit of consciousness will undergo certain experiences that are karmically necessary in order to *further the spiritual growth of the Soul.* During the incarnated period, or "earthly life," the unit of consciousness will most probably be unaware of his true spiritual nature due to the necessary dense vibrational consciousness/reality of the Physical Plane of existence.

We can view spiritual growth as REMEMBRANCE, as you know ... a process during which the person, by the use of various esoteric techniques, REMEMBERS that he is essentially a spiritual being or individualized unit of Pure Consciousness. Through utilization of these various methods and techniques, the person will gain much more in the long run than by any activity centered in the dynamics of the Physical Plane ... i.e. harvesting money, working like a dog, engagement in manipulative power struggles. This is because of the fact that, in the end, everything is simple and springs from the distilled Pure Essence of Being and not "doing," as you know. It is unfortunate that so many people in your realm are engaged in putting themselves through needless pain and "suffering" (as the Buddhists say), when the simple and direct access of only a portion of their spiritual identity will enrich their lives beyond any of their material expectations.

Elaborate on "due to the nature and dynamics of manifestation, Pure Joy underlies the whole bailiwick."

Well, now you're talking!! Let's have some fun!! If we consider that the nature of Pure Consciousness is PURE IS-NESS, then we can see that, in order for manifestation to occur, reality/consciousness constructs must be conceived of and projected from the Field of Pure Consciousness. These CONSTRUCTS are comprised of CONSCIOUSNESS ONLY and must conform to Natural Laws that deal with manifestation ... i.e. there are certain ways that things just naturally work due to the nature of things ("that's the way things IS").

Now here's some juicy meat for you - Joy (or Bliss) is the underlying Nature of manifested Reality because the simple dynamics of broadcasting the realms through the "OM" vibration means that, hence, EVERYTHING IN MANIFESTATION IS SIMPLY VIBRATION. The lower frequencies of this vibration are all the heavy dense (tamasic) things and objects of the Physical Plane. *The highest manifestation of this vibration is merely bliss ...* i.e. the highest manifested expression of VIBRATION is "felt" or "experienced" as Bliss. Bliss is a high vibrational consciousness/energy, naturally expressing in every single extant thing.

This is why when we expand the consciousness of the individual, he will eventually begin to experience Bliss because HE IS BLISS, essentially. BLISS IS HIS NATURAL CONDITION, at the highest level of experience and manifestation. If we consider that the individualized expression of Pure Consciousness is going about, daily, those things and practices which will eventually bring it to a place of pure bliss, we can see that Bliss is merely its already occurring, natural or Innate condition. What is clouding the individual's experience of his own Bliss-State is merely *over-involvement with the mental and emotional components and over-externalization of attention.*

When the individual reaches a point of evolution/unfoldment where he simply starts to meditate or INTERNALIZE his attention, he will naturally, with time, discover this Bliss for himself as IT IS ALWAYS THERE, a part of his essential nature. It must simply "come forth" or appear with time because it is his already extant "core self" and cannot remain "un-experienced" forever.

Speak to the concept "all of Creation is a dance."

And there you have it! It's a simple thing really, always overcomplicated by the lower mind in its ceaseless analytical activities. If we consider the essence of dance, we can see that it is spontaneous (more or less) movement CENTERED IN THE MOMENT and conceived in FLOW. Good dancers merely flow from one spot to another, EFFORTLESSLY AND JOYOUSLY. Now, one might think that this means that no discipline or training are required, and, for a certain type of experience, this is true. However, when training has been undertaken and then integrated so that the individual may actualize the "form training" from a place of consciousness or flow, then we have a condition that could be described as Pure Flow or (surprise!) Pure Consciousness in Expression.

While it is true that many people in your realm attempt to "bully" form in very controlling and restrictive ways, what could be said is that *form must be allowed to simply express of its own generation.* This is what we know as "T'ai Chi doing T'ai Chi" or "the music plays itself." If we conceptualize the manifested realms of existence as a gigantic dance in process, then we can see that the purpose of this dance is EXPRESSION OF JOY. There is no other purpose for the manifestation of Pure Consciousness.

If everything manifested is a dance, then the dancers are engaged in a process of ENJOYMENT. One may switch partners or one may stumble and fall, but what is occurring is merely a DANCE OF JOY so, if one falls, one just joins right back in saying, with a laugh, "Oh, well!" If we conceptualize this dance as a square dance, then we can see that every dancer, or element, *has his or her part to play in the dance in order for it to become Complete or Whole.*

You might think that the dance will then be limited to one FORM, but no! The form will merely metamorphose and soon everyone will be engaged joyously in a different dance. Therefore the dance is a wonderful metaphor for Creation, as it expresses Unity through FORM INVOLVED IN CHANGE. Those that would think that the dance must remain static would not understand the basic nature of the manifested realms, STILLNESS IN MOTION ... and in this basic nature the "stillness" or Spirit is constantly engaged in *creative generation of new form*, or "change."

While it might be true that many people in your realm try (and succeed) to complicate this simple dynamic, once again, the intrinsic simplicity of All That Exists must be stressed because what can be complicated in the expression of the JOY that springs from the "Pure Beingness" of the Absolute?

Discuss "Unconditional Love."

Well, we might say, once again, that Unconditional Love is the only game in town. While it is true that the inhabitants of your realm are fairly confused about the nature of LOVE, we could say that it manifests as ENERGY/CONSCIOUSNESS and can merely be viewed as the "attractive glue" that holds everything together. When we are examining love from the perspective of the Physical Plane of existence, we can see that it is thought of as an *emotion* ... this is most definitely not the case, although there are emotional components that accessorize it.

One might consider love to be a FUNDAMENTAL PROPERTY of the manifested realms, as it is the resonance of one element of consciousness with another one in a dance of Unity realization. This means that each "separate" thing will find commonality and resonance with various other elements of consciousness due to the intrinsic nature of the integral connection between All That Exists.

However, due to ENERGETIC DYNAMICS of the "lower bodies" or consciousness vehicles of man, the essential Unity underlying all of Creation is often not perceived by the individualized unit of consciousness and, instead, a condition of separation and competition is believed to be the Ultimate Condition of Reality. This can be best described, as Itzhak Bentov has done, as a holdover or remnant of the Animal Reality ... kill or be killed, survival of the fittest, etc., and it was useful for Beings at a certain level of experience or learning. However, in the human, this then expresses as FEAR and sort of gets in the way and mucks up just about everything that you can possibly think of. This is, of course, why various spiritual disciplines advocate the REMOVAL OF FEAR, through one method or another, from the consciousness.

Speak to the unfoldment of the "Love consciousness" during this New Age and what it will mean to us all.

As it is the case that LOVE IS EVERYWHERE NOW, the "New Age" will merely shift the emphasis of human life and experience to a simple question: "Where is the Way of Love?" The old ways, steeped in fear and power/manipulation will be gone ... those that attempt to use them will find that they merely get NOWHERE FAST. As it is the case that the whole culture is, at this point, still rather enmeshed in this Fear/Pain deely-wobber, we can easily comprehend that there will be a period of GREAT DENSE VIBRATION for many people now presently incarnate in the Physical Plane. Those that are open to the "new way" (actually, of course, an Ancient, Old Way) of Love will find that their lives are filled up .... they will have more of "the good stuff" than they know what to do with.

This entire shift of energy/consciousness in your sphere, unfolding up to and then taking off at the Great Moment of Stillness, will be quite the wonderful thing and is experienced by *every single manifested universe at a particular "Universal Rest Point."* There is, of course, NOTHING AT ALL to be concerned with during these times, as the essence of everyone is that they are currently, and will remain, an IMMORTAL SPIRITUAL BEING. So the "doings" and "goings-on" in the Physical Plane of existence are merely that ... just for experience or FUN, if you wanna look at it that way.

There are those that will say that these times are "heavy" or "dangerous" or "fraught with peril," but once again, when viewed from the individualized and collective spiritual, this is A BUNCH OF HOOEY!! This time can be viewed as merely a "transitional game" and the best result will be had by RELAXING INTO IT WITHOUT FEAR OR CONCERN. This enables the individual to "go with the flow" of whatever is spontaneously occurring.

Individuals will notice, at this time, that there is much global and personal "cleansing" or removal of low-vibrational energy going on and, once again, merely "go with the flow" and RIDE THE TIGER. As with other cleansings, the person will sometimes be tired, or "crabby" (irritable), giggly, sick, joyous, blissful, mean ... you get the point ... it's the ol' "PAIRS OF OPPOSITES" AGAIN! Don't make it harder than it needs to be ... merely "go forth and groove"!!

Discuss the concept "actualization of individual Joy."

While in physical incarnation, the individualized unit of consciousness can best actualize Joy in his/her life by merely "doing what comes naturally" and WHAT THEY ARE DRAWN TO. It is the case that most people are very far away from this and are engaged in performance of conditioned behavior, which would include things that they "should" do according to cultural/societal norms.

When it becomes apparent, usually after many lives, to the human unit of consciousness that this approach is "not cutting the nut," so to speak, they begin to seek out those ways and things that they are more DRAWN TO and it is helpful at this point to release or "let go of" any negative conditionings that are attempting to "hold them back" ... i.e. "you can't get what you want," "I really should do this," etc. In the Swimming Sea of Consciousness, the individualized essence of Supreme Consciousness is not "supposed" to go through life fettered in chains and dreading existence or "suffering," as the Buddhists say.

When we consider that THERE IS NOTHING ELSE EXISTING BUT AN OCEAN OF PURE JOY, it is unfortunate that this is apparent to or "Realized" by only a few individuals at this point in time because of the nature of physical incarnation and its persistent focus on externals, which merely amount to the Dance of Consciousness. If the individualized essence becomes fascinated by this dance, and forgets that the dance exists for his pleasure/experience, THEN THE TROUBLE BEGINS.

As has been mentioned, it is merely because of certain mental/emotional factors, which are obscuring or "clouding" the realization of internal/external Joy, that the human unit of consciousness is not ALWAYS aware of his True Nature. When it is time for the unit of consciousness to realize his True Nature, he then becomes aware of ways, methods and practices which basically refine the cerebrospinal system and allow him to see for himself that Joy is Everywhere, it's Everywhere!

So, obviously then, there is never any reason to "wait" for Joy to manifest in the future?

JOY IS MERELY ALL THERE IS, THERE IS NOTHING ELSE AT ALL! Once again, it is merely over-involvement with the mental and emotional components that is causing people to believe they are existing in a realm of suffering when instead PARADISE IS EVERYWHERE NOW. Why wait around? Why take time to hone the spiritual bodies? *Merely relax to the fullest degree possible now, secure in the knowledge that there is now, and never has been, anything at all to fear.* What can there be to fear in an Oceanic Rippling Expanse of Pure Love, Bliss, and Joy?

The mental and emotional components of human beings, which can be conceptualized as merely lower expressions of Being, are characterized by POLARITY or extremes of vibration. This is why the Buddha said, "Always follow the Middle Way." In the "centering" of the individual's mental and emotional components, the Light of Spirit just shines on down through and ILLUMINATES the entire energetic structure of the consciousness unit and then it can readily see that it has merely been engaged in putting *itself* through some "DENSE VIBRATION," so to speak, for a multitude of lifetimes. This does not mean that this "experiential life" is not a part of the natural condition of human beings, it is, just as the evolution of the cerebrospinal system is a natural process and occurrence.

How about some "tips" for the personal actualization of Joy?

THE PURE JOY OF BEING IS THE ESSENCE OF MANIFESTED "BEINGNESS" AND PERVADES ALL NOW!! This about sums it up ... there is nothing else but Joy and all other perspectives are illusory, or based in IGNORANCE of energy or spiritual matters. If we consider that there is nothing but Pure Joy, then we can harvest several "big tips" for actualizing the experience of Joy for the condensed expression of Pure Consciousness:

1. BE HERE NOW. Don't be off goofing around with some EXPERIENCE of the past - who wants or needs it? Watch DOGS, they don't waste their time with this goofiness!!

2. GO TOWARD WHAT YOU ARE DRAWN TO. What is the use in doing things for any other reason, like say - MONEY? The person might end up with a lot of money and not one bit of personal satisfaction - you decide which is better.

3. DO NOT ACCEPT ANY LIMITATION AT ALL REGARDLESS OF WHAT QUARTER IT COMES FROM. Let's say a "spiritual teacher" lays something on you like, "You must do it like this or it's not Pure." *Give me a break!!* This is the biggest bunch of self-aggrandizing HOOEY that I've ever heard and it should be consistently fought because it is the basic nature of daily cultural life in the U.S., so IT'S THE SAME OLD THANG!! Those that are trying to share something of value with non-attachment will merely say "try this and see if it works for you."

4. HAVE LOTS OF LAUGHTER AND FUN NOW!! Why wait to hone the spiritual bodies? Why wait till you "solve all the mysteries"? The nature of Spirit or Soul is that it is *laughing now with the sheer fun of existence*, it ain't sitting around brooding about this or that. Always have as much fun and laugh as much as possible because this is the way of the higher realities ... the misperception of LACK and non-perfection that pervades your realm is merely that - MISPERCEPTION. It is eventually transcended by every single condensed expression of PC but until that point - *laugh now, not later*.

5. SEEK THOSE THINGS THAT GIVE YOU JOY NOW - ignore those things that give you "pain" or dissatisfaction. As it is the case that "pain" or "suffering" is of the mind and not of the Essential Nature, we can see that, like with other "high things," one can groove by merely *according with the Joy that exists now*, like the process of according with the Perfection that exists now!!

Discuss in more detail the nature of the "star-being" (this refers to consciousness that is physically expressed as a star, in our case, the Sun).

It could be said that the star-being is the localized representative of Pure Consciousness or God. This, obviously, can also be viewed as a CONDENSATION of Pure Consciousness on a local level. So the star-being serves the region of its physical location. All minor beings are contained within its consciousness ... i.e. the operating dynamics of consciousness are modular in nature ... bigger unit of consciousness containing smaller.

While it is true that the star being can be thought of as existing at a highly developed level of consciousness, this in no way implies that the individual human being cannot access these levels of existence. As Itzhak Bentov, as well as many others, has said, the nature of manifested consciousness is that it is HOLOGRAPHIC in expression. This means that each "chunk" of consciousness contains all of the information contained in the Whole.

While this is a very good model for what is occurring, it is a very difficult thing, as I have previously stressed, to comprehend or grasp from the perspective of the Physical Plane. It might be compared to the dynamic that is seen at play in many older people. Initially, as youngsters, they believe life to be about striving, accomplishing, and achieving material ends. As maturity dawns, they perceive that this is a dead end street, as it were, that whereas there lies some satisfaction in it, all levels of the deepest satisfaction originate in NON-MATERIAL REALITY.

When we consider this as applied to the star being, we see that each unit of consciousness is constantly growing and unfolding (or evolving) to greater and greater levels of expression of all its Innate Possibilities, which are Infinite and Unbounded by definition. When seen from the perspective of the Physical Plane, the star-being demonstrates the basic quality of giving or Love ... as you have noticed, all it does is SHINE, SHINE, SHINE all the time, presenting the physical worlds with warmth and light. It cannot be said that the star-being is doing this for any purpose other than the PURE EXPRESSION OF THE UNBOUNDED JOY OF EXISTENCE.

This is one of the great, misunderstood secrets ... everything, as it actualizes its own expression or level of Joyousness, automatically "gives" or provides something of value to the manifested creation. This is a simple thing really, and it is routinely overcomplicated in realms such as yours where the lower mind can "get at it" and sort of muck things up by over-analyzing. EVERYTHING IS SIMPLE, FOR EVERYTHING IS SIMPLY CONSCIOUSNESS! This is the mantra and the watchword of the coming times.

Some thoughts on "relaxing into life"?

Relaxing into life is the simplest and easiest thing that anyone could ever do, for it merely requires that they BE PRESENT wherever and whenever they are involved in any experiential circumstance of the Physical Plane. Tension, being of the lower mind, is merely a "blocker" or "obstruction" of higher states of experiential consciousness, and is to be discarded as soon as the individualized essence of Pure Consciousness can actualize the realization that there is NOTHING TO FEAR WHATSOEVER IN THE EXPERIENCES AND MODALITIES OF EXISTENCE.

If there is no fear, then there can be Flow and this includes various "vibrations" or "frequencies of flow" that can be also characterized as aspects of the Essential Nature of man and All That Is. Coming from a perspective of tension, the individualized unit of consciousness perceives LACK AND DANGER all around him for he incorrectly assumes the physical existence to be the only existence. This is a sad error that can be best described by the term "ignorance" ... the person is ignorant on a conscious level of his True Nature and so is constrained to view the objects and circumstances of the Physical Plane as his "true home."

The essence of the transformative process known variously as Enlightenment, "salvation," satori, or Self-realization is one of REMEMBRANCE, as has been previously discussed. This means that the individual merely remembers what has always been. No big deal. It is merely the misperception that there is something to "struggle against" that is currently causing energy dynamics in your sphere to swirl around madly like a badger with his tail in a trap!

While it could be said that those who are engaged in "struggle behavior" are merely trying to do what they can according to their perceptions, in the coming days this mode of behavior will prove ineffective as the entire range of energy/consciousness in your realm is shifting to a higher vibrational rate. Of course, this shift is the genesis of the turmoil currently being felt in your sphere, both on a global and personal level. I would think that many of your fellow humans would get tired of this "struggle thang" after awhile and decide that maybe there really was something to "relaxing into" life after all! While it is true that those who retain the "grasping hook" view of life will find that things become somewhat more trying for them in these coming days, the essence of the Physical Plane is that it is a SPHERE OF EXPERIENCE in which NO ONE IS ESSENTIALLY HARMED.

The necessity of continued experience in the Physical Plane (i.e. further incarnations) can be greatly shortened by engagement in the esoteric practices already known in every culture and religious setting.

How about some thoughts on Bliss?

It is unnecessary, once again, to unfold the various spiritual components present in the human being to experience the highest Bliss .... JUST RELAX FULLY AND COMPLETELY NOW. It's easy, it's simple .... *it already exists at the core of your Being, so this is why you merely relax into it!!*

This has been a wild week ... commentary?

Well, what one might say, Mark, is that it just keeps getting wilder and wilder! Probably the most misunderstood aspects of spiritual growth (in your realm) include the aspects of EXPANSION, FREEDOM, AND DUTY.

To elaborate, expansion of consciousness is merely greater access to the NATURAL STATE OF PERMANENT CONSCIOUSNESS OF THE INDIVIDUAL, and is attained by various means, including (but not limited to) good deeds, treating other human beings well, service to other humans beings, etc. You are beginning to understand that these are all kriyas ("kriya" means "action" in Sanskrit - this could be informally taken to mean "spiritual action"). Kundalini kriyas, of all sorts, including T'ai Chi and Chi Kung, are the rocket-ship to the stars, so to speak ... and when combined with the consciousness force present behind practices that have been utilized by many, many aspirants through linear time, these things are extremely potent methods of unfoldment or evolution.

Freedom is the NATURAL CONDITION of all condensed expressions of Pure Consciousness and, as such, *is not something that can be taken away!* Everyone is always free, at all times, and so access to Freedom is the realization that YOU ARE ALREADY FREE and can simply use well known methods ... ignoring things you are not drawn to, *letting things go* ... especially unwanted mental things, in order to experience the maximum amount of Freedom. One could say that Freedom is like a river that runs unchecked .... it might go here, it might go there, but it goes wherever it wants, with flow and response.

Duty is merely the spontaneous desire or "pull" that arises as the cerebrospinal system is refined and will vary due to the nature of the individualized unit of consciousness. Some will want to WRITE, wouldn't *you* say?, and some will want more close personal "touching" methods of service. It's simple ... just go to whatever you are drawn to and focus your energies there, as that is NATURALLY RIGHT for you and it feels good, too!

If we consider that condensed expressions of Consciousness are always Free, and we conceptualize this Freedom as being COMPLETE AND TOTAL, unbounded, NO LIMITATIONS, then we can understand that most cannot even perceive the true nature of their own already extant freedom!! This is a sticky wicket, so to speak, because it is not until an individual has attained a certain level of, say it with me now, CEREBROSPINAL DEVELOPMENT, that they will begin to access levels of consciousness in which they start to have a hint of this condition of freedom. So "you are free now" is merely a statement of fact ... everyone is always free, as the condition is not one that can be taken away.

When the individualized expression of Pure Consciousness has reached a state of cerebrospinal development that it can begin to have certain experiences and perceptions, it will discover ON ITS OWN the nature of the depth of its freedom. Until this time, there are certain methods which can help in accessing this Freedom, and these include: *ignoring (or letting go of)* things that you are not drawn to or feel a connection with, *visualization* of desired goals and results (use of creative imagination), *utilization of various techniques* to further the personal unfoldment, *advice and counsel* of those who have traveled this (or their own) path before, *living more from a place of "Being,"* from which will spring "proper" action, or action which contains the essence of FLOW.

Speak about worry?

THERE IS NOW, AND NEVER HAS BEEN, ANYTHING TO WORRY ABOUT AT ALL! Worry merely depletes energy, energy that can be better used for other things. In a Swimming Sea of Pure Consciousness only, we can start to realize that everything is completely PERFECT AS IT IS, whether or not we understand this intellectually. My advice *always* will be ... merely relax into any situation that you find yourself in and find enjoyment. Those that are able to do this will find their lives going remarkably smoothly, which will often be a puzzle to those observing from the "outside."

Maybe we can view the state of worry like a giant tree that has suddenly decided that it must uproot itself and become a squirrel, instead of merely standing firm and Being as it would naturally Be. *Just do what you are drawn to and everything else will simply take care of itself.* Remarkable concept, eh? ... and one that is consistently fought in the culture as a whole. ALL WORRIES ARE GROUNDLESS, ALL CONCERNS TURN TO DUST when the essence of the spiritual reality becomes clear.

Speak on this concept ... "there is never any need for worry, serenity can be had at any time."

Very good! Yes it is true that there is NEVER anything to worry about for what can go wrong in an all-enveloping Sea of Pure Consciousness? It may seem that those that finally accept this simple concept find themselves in a place of diminished autonomy, but in fact the opposite is true. When one accepts the reality of this precept, then one "relaxes into" whatever place he may find himself with great ease ... SERENITY. It is only the pursuit of "illusory" things that cause the mind to become ensnared in worry and the incorrect perception of lack.

Unfortunately, in your culture, the sense of lack is a highly ingrained thought-form that pervades the group consciousness, and this leaves us in the unenviable circumstance of NOT BEING ABLE TO SEE THE NOSE THAT'S ON OUR FACE, as it were. It is only through individual effort that slowly, slowly the group consciousness is changed to reflect the simple fact that everything is Bliss and there is no lack anywhere. The acceptance of this fact brings about the completion of the operating dynamics of the Physical Plane ... i.e. when one accepts this, he naturally starts to experience greater abundance in his life in many ways. This is merely a simple Law of Existence or Being, as it were.

More on Serenity?

When it is understood, finally, that there is NO LACK and everything is unfolding PERFECTLY, what is there to be afraid of? One can then choose complete serenity, or more appropriately said, *one merely "falls into" complete Serenity.* It is not a dynamic of thought, it is a realized or experiential thing.

Can you illuminate the "right brain/left brain" dynamic?

The nature of the right brain/left brain situation is such that one can observe its dynamic in many natural occurrences and processes, as you might suspect. One could say that the right brain is the essentially "creative" or "expressive" aspect and the left brain is the essentially "logical" brain aspect. Now, when imbalances occur in these two hemispheres we observe specific conditions and workings at play.

You might think of the situation with a plant that lives wild in nature. The plant must provide for its survival in the way that it knows how. In the plant kingdom, this involves relying on relationships with other plants, insects, animals, the sun, rain, etc.

These things are not under the DIRECT control of the plant and so the plant merely selects for these things by natural processes ... i.e., the seeds of the plant will grow well only in those sites that "fit the bill" in terms of its needs.

If we contemplate the life of the plant, we can see that this process of selection of growth sites is analogous with the left brain dynamic of the human unit of consciousness which is concerned with survival concerns of various types. The plant's right brain analogue would be its display of foliage or flowers in various forms which would amount to an EXPRESSION of the plant's essential energy nature.

This analogy, although somewhat distant, is a good one to demonstrate that these two aspects of consciousness ... i.e. SURVIVAL and EXPRESSION, formulate a Yin-Yang dynamic as does the right brain/left brain dynamic. One might say, and in fact one does, that this type of relationship can be seen in all things that are manifested. You will think that maybe we have gone far afield from the initial question ... however it is very important to see the relationships and congruencies in all of nature.

As to possible imbalances that can occur in-between the hemispheres, it can be generally said that in the United States today most people are unbalanced toward the left side, meaning here that they are concerned with the "logical" aspects of SURVIVAL. The essence of EXPRESSION is thought to be frivolous and so is discarded at some point in young adulthood in favor of the ceaseless and repetitive questing after money, fame, jobs, security, love of a romantic nature and other things. One can then see that these things do not provide deep satisfaction and individuals may come to realize this as they age and begin to seek internally and externally.

The completion of internal searches such as the one that you are involved in is that the individual will come to realize that there is no need to become concerned with mere SURVIVAL in a realm of PURE ABUNDANCE, and instead what is really desired is EXPRESSION. When it is comprehended at the level of the soul that this is the nature of fulfillment and basic satisfaction, the individual will begin to change his mode of operation and try to establish a basic level of survival on top of which he will incorporate the dynamic of expression of some sort.

This then leads to the final stage in which the individual realizes that what must be done is EXPRESSION as a first rule and then SURVIVAL needs are easily filled. One can see that the essence of expression is contained within the right brain so that, in the States, we are horribly unbalanced in the direction of the left brain.

Do you have any commentary concerning T'ai Chi and Chi Kung ... importance of form verses importance of elements such as lightness and flow?

Well, we might consider T'ai Chi to be an art that will eventually grant to the practitioner the greatest gifts and secrets of the Universe. While it is true that T'ai Chi and Chi Kung are not routinely practiced at this point in time in the United States, this is rapidly changing. You are well aware of the magnificence of this practice and its possible benefits to those who are diligent and persevere in the practice.

While it is true that form is an important element, form is not the "thang," as it were, in the end. It is true that the mental framework or dwelling place while performing the discipline is paramount. This means that one needs to be in the proper frame of mind (i.e. calm, still thoughtlessness) for the discipline to provide the greatest benefits AND experiences. After a period of time of practice, one will find that the movements flow naturally, with little or no effort or thought, and the deeper essences of the practice start to come to the forefront. These include Bliss, Joy, Peace, fullness, flexibility, etc. and normally require some time to develop.

You will find that the essence of T'ai Chi can be described as the completion of the ancient saying, "He who does not walk in the sun, walks in the ...." While it is true that one might complete this is many fashions, it could be said that perhaps the best fashion would be one in which it could be used to solve the most riddles. The most riddles can be solved by the simplest means. The simplest means can be found by looking to the easiest place. When one has found the easiest place, one has found the Tao ... effortless and wonderful, flowing and stress-less. While it can be seen in daily life that most people are busily driving themselves crazy with the many things that they must do, it can be found that those who live the fullest lives are those that take the slowest route.

Would "shade" solve the riddle?

Well yes, I think that would complete the limerick nicely!

What information do you have regarding various ongoing things of interest?

If we consider that everything is always unfolding perfectly, then we can see with great clarity that there are no IMPERFECT things anywhere at any time. As this is the case, then it can be said that those things that are occurring, whether or not they are perceived as "good" by the individualized essence of Pure Consciousness, are working toward the GREATER EXPRESSION OF THE INNATE NATURE OF BLISS AND RADIANCE. There is now, and never will be, any reason to fret or be concerned over the unfoldment of events in the Physical Plane.

Speak to the "Joy of Pure Being."

Well, of course, what we can always say concerning the Joy of Pure Being is it's EVERYWHERE AND EVER PRESENT ... there is not a space that can be found that is not pervaded and permeated by shear, Pure Joy. *There is simply nothing else.* While it might be the case that those who would argue against the possibility of the Pure Joy of Being could be considered ignorant, we could also say that the energetic dynamics of the Physical Plane of existence are such that there is little likelihood that many people will realize the pervasive nature of Pure Joy (Bliss, Love, Truth, etc.) except by DEVELOPMENT OF THE CEREBROSPINAL SYSTEM through the utilization of one or more methods.

As you have begun to see the wonderful states of consciousness that become apparent once this process has started, we can perceive the importance of more people becoming convinced to "give yoga a try" (or T'ai Chi or both) because the *payoff is much greater than they will initially have the ability to even conceive.* This is why it is good that you like to talk about these various practices with people, as your realm is very pervaded by the type of thought-forms that encourage people to be "more busy" and take less time for rest and spiritual discipline.

This, as you know, is merely a conditioning and can be easily overcome if the individualized unit of consciousness will merely take the initiative to explore the spiritual realms. When they do, they will find that everything is merely "grooviness" or Pure Consciousness, and there is now and never has been ANYTHING TO FEAR AT ALL! THERE IS ONLY PURE JOY!

Esoteric Practice

"Traveler, what is it you seek here,
as this is not your True Home?"
Unknown

The many and diverse cultures of the world have all originated various spiritual disciplines which in the past have largely been kept secret and reserved for use only by a very few members of the elite. These practices would include Kundalini Yoga, Taoist Yoga and T'ai Chi, esoteric Tibetan Buddhist practice, American Indian practices, South Sea Island practices, esoteric Christian practice .... the list goes on and on. The fundamental purpose of these practices, if they have any merit, is the **refinement of the human cerebrospinal system**. It is through this refinement that the individualized Essence of Pure Consciousness that *is* a human being can gain access, while in physical incarnation, to his Original or Being Nature, which is unchanging and *remains as it always has been.*

The culmination of esoteric practice is often said to be Enlightenment, salvation, satori, or Self-Realization (there are many different terms describing the same place of Being), and it might clear away some of the confusion to stress that these terms describe *an already extant state*. Everyone, at a certain level of Being, is already perfectly illumined, Whole and content. The esoteric practices, through the refinement of the cerebrospinal system, merely allow the practitioner to gain **conscious** access to the Fundamental Condition which is already his.

One does not get to this place of Realization by over-striving but instead by *relaxing* more and more into life until everything just effortlessly flows. Our culture, being basically one of **struggle and competition,** does not have a handle on this and people continue to mistakenly believe that the road to happiness lies in *striving* of one type or another. But it could be said that the road to happiness lies, ultimately, *in simply **Being**,* for what struggle, hardship or pain can there be in a state of Pure Being?

Today, esoteric practices that were once secret disciplines like Kundalini Yoga (Kriya Yoga, Siddha Yoga, etc.) are becoming readily available to the general public. Additionally, Chi Kung, T'ai Chi, and Reiki (a "hands-on" method of healing or energy transfer revealed to Dr. Mikao Usui in the last century) are becoming widespread. This information is becoming available because the entire spectrum of consciousness in our realm is rapidly shifting upwards due to naturally occurring, scientific dynamics taking place in the physical universe (culminating in what I call The Great Moment of Stillness - more on this later).

As I have been engaged in esoteric practice for awhile, I utilize the channeling process to gain various types of information that is pertinent to the various practices. Much of this information is quite fascinating and helpful. I have also included some channeled information on cerebrospinal refinement in this chapter, as this concept is very new to some people and this helps to further illuminate the practices which are the "rocket ships" of consciousness.

Discuss the importance of the development or refinement of the cerebrospinal system.

Well, it all boils down to this ... the cerebrospinal system of man is the "consciousness interface" that is present or "built into" the human unit of consciousness. Without development of the cerebrospinal system, no advanced interchange of consciousness is possible because this is the "telephone," so to speak, between the differing levels of consciousness and the "waking" mind of the human. It is necessary that the human utilize one or another of the various and wonderful methods of development of the cerebrospinal system that is found in every culture ... everything from T'ai Chi to yoga to going forth doing good ... there are many different routes to accomplish the development.

The "scientific methods," such as yoga, can be thought of as rocket ships of transformation, cutting much time off the experiences necessary in the "evolutionary" route (the Chain of Lives of reincarnation). However, the unfoldment of the Innate Nature, culminating in Self-realization, is a NATURAL process and will just

NATURALLY occur, given enough linear time. Those who would enjoy the exploration of higher reaches of consciousness will find it wise to listen to the yogis of all lands and employ some of their methods.

Discuss human potentiality.

Ah ha! Interesting subject! One could say that human potential, like the unlimited potential of any individualized unit of consciousness or soul, IS AS VAST AS THE SKY. What is engaged in limiting the expression of human potentiality is the potentiality itself. You will find that those who are able to access the higher, spiritual nature of themselves begin to transcend the conditionings and group consciousness thought-forms that are keeping the bulk of humanity in SELF-IMPOSED chains. It could be said that everyone is a fountain of potentiality waiting to erupt.

Do not think that it is always easy for one living incarnate in the Physical Plane of existence to develop their potentials, for it is not. It requires some large measure of persistence and courage for one will encounter misunderstanding and rejection from many quarters while in the process. The simple fact is that each individualized human unit of Supreme Consciousness contains within itself the Whole and the implied potentiality of that Wholeness. The universe is a HOLOGRAM, as Itzhak Bentov so wonderfully points out. You will find that as you explore the vastness of yourself, many VERY interesting things will occur and will subsequently be difficult if not impossible to relate to those who have not developed their cerebrospinal systems. I would say that the essence of human potentiality can be described by this maxim: "He who laughs first, laughs last."

Discuss meditation.

Meditation is the ACTIVE PRACTICE OF EXPERIENCING YOUR "BEING" NATURE by the cessation (largely) of the activities of the mind so that the higher Pure Essence can merely shine through! MEDITATION IS NOT AN ACTIVITY OF STRIVING!! It is, inherently, an activity of *relaxing into that which you already are.* This means ... you are that now, not later! This means, that which you have always been and is not different in essence from your "personality" self; it is merely a higher expression.

The pieces of the puzzle of Enlightenment can be discovered to be no "puzzle" at all ... it is merely THAT WHICH YOU ARE NOW AT A HIGHER LEVEL. This is why all good meditation teachers do not stress completely "shutting down the mind" but instead *relaxing into whatever experience you are having.* If one relaxes enough, one merely RELAXES into their Essential or Innate Nature. It's easy, it's simple ... it occurs of it's own accord if given enough linear time ... i.e. never forget that it is a natural process - not supernatural!

What information do you have regarding being in the presence of spiritual energies and the transmission of these energies, from a place or a person?

It is the case that those people who are open to associating with any person or event where the "big vibration" is present, and to continually re-immersing themselves in this type of energy, are the ones that will experience the MOST RAPID SPIRITUAL GROWTH. We can see that this is a *highly recommended activity,* because the energy merely "works on you" and takes care of things. Many people are too quick to "back off" from this type of contact when they start to experience the tiredness and emotional and other releases that are naturally generated. The tiredness and releases are merely symptomatic of the way this high vibrational energy assists the individualized condensation of Pure Consciousness.

GOING INTO THIS TYPE OF ENERGY IS UNBELIEVABLY BENEFICIAL, and will result in a shortened time of unfoldment. Since lack of God-awareness or, to put it another way, knowledge of the Buddha Nature (same thing!) is considered to be suffering, then it is useful to merely "go into" the spiritual energies and let them do what they will with you - it is an ENTIRELY BENEFICENT PROCESS, which the individual is "seeking" or "desiring" now - there is no "down side," from an individual or collective basis.

What this means is this - where you are all "going" is exactly where you *are now* at a higher level of consciousness and is a place of COMPLETE CONTENTMENT, JOY, LOVE, BLISS, PEACE, and any other non-polar high attribute you can think of. *It is a very groovy place of self-completeness and no lack.* There will be little or no dependence on externals for a sense of love, joy, and contentment. It will not be necessary for the events unfolding in the manifested realms to occur in any certain way. Instead, you will merely be IN THE FLOW of them and will be able to meet all bodily needs (food, shelter, recreation, comfort, etc.) easily and quickly. All higher needs - EXISTENCE, CONSCIOUSNESS, and BLISS (this includes all the Innate "feeling" qualities like Love, etc.) - will be perceived as originating or unfolding from WITHIN YOUR OWN BEING, so no big deal - you've already got the goodies! It is merely the over-involvement of the person's consciousness or Innate Essence with the senses and mental and emotional things that is leading them to mistakenly believe that they do not already have ALL that they essentially need.

Is "normal" Reiki a lower vibrational energy than the other "symbol-based" energies?

It could be said that "normal" Reiki is the basic unit of Reiki consciousness and the other energies are modifications of this basic unit. "Normal" Reiki is perfectly suited to the general improvement and maintenance of the OVERALL health of the individual, while the other "frequencies" are more specific to different areas and dynamics occurring throughout the individual. You would do well to use all Reiki energies currently available to you (there are more), as all of them will assist you in the most rapid transition through this time.

Did Reiki come from or has it been associated with Tibetan Buddhism?

What one could say is that Reiki is associated with Tibetan Buddhism through the shared wisdom and energetic dynamics of the Buddha. The Tibetan Buddhists utilize many very similar techniques to that which is today known as Reiki, however it cannot be said with certainty just exactly what the origins of the Reiki form are.

Speak more concerning the connection between Reiki and Tibetan Buddhism.

It could be said that the Buddha lives in both Tibetan Buddhists and the practitioners of Reiki. While it is the case that those associated with Reiki have an ongoing energetic relationship with the Buddha, they do not directly have a relationship with those practicing Tibetan Buddhism today. Tibetan Buddhists and Reiki practitioners are brothers in the Buddha, as it were.

This is likened to two different pathways up to the top of a mountain ... the mountain is the same, only the approach is different. Same thing with Reiki practitioners and Tibetan Buddhists. While it is true that many Reiki practitioners associate Reiki with Tibetan Buddhism, the best that can be said is that the essence of Tibetan Buddhism is embraced by those who administer the Reiki energies in discarnate form. Now many individual Reiki practitioners will be drawn to Tibetan Buddhism, but this is because of its intrinsic merit and not because of any special DIRECT energy connections, other than the obvious one between all beings.

While it could be said that you will find those who practice Tibetan Buddhism to be very interesting, some of the approaches and philosophical positions will remain generally alien to the western mind, and like the Dalai Lama says, will only cause mental conflict, something to be avoided.

Was the emerald green rectangle that I saw while sending distance Reiki associated with Reiki or the Reiki ray?

Well, one could say that the Reiki ray is, by definition, associated with the Emerald ray. The green color you saw was definitely associated with the process and energetic dynamics of Reiki usage. While it is true that Reiki cannot be discovered in daily life by the examination of the aspects of the Physical Plane of existence, it is the case that it pervades all anyway, merely at a higher level of consciousness vibration. Access to Reiki energies is a simple thing, really, and is to be promoted by those that possess Reiki and understand its potency.

At a certain level of existence, the utilization of symbols and other means of "access" is unnecessary, as the individualized unit of consciousness merely intuitively understands how to access these higher frequencies. For those in the early stages of awakening, Reiki is an invaluable tool ... powerful, fun, and "not of this earth" in such a way as to convince even the most hide-bound skeptic that the possibility of other realities or modes of existence is very real.

Discuss physical exercise.

What we could say is that physical exercise is very, very important during times of intensive energy work, such as what you have been experiencing, because it allows energy flows to be integrated into the physical reality. When we consider that the majority of Americans do not get enough physical exercise to begin with, we can see that it is a rare thing that an "energy worker" especially actualizes enough exercise, as they are frequently prone to be sedentary and more concerned with strictly spiritual matters. Physical activity is good, and merely works to FURTHER INTEGRATE PSYCHIC ENERGIES INTO THE PHYSICAL BODY, as well as maintain the circulatory system and grant the exerciser a general level of good physical health.

As you know from your studies, the mind-body matrix is closely linked together ... work on the body, work on the mind. This is also true in reverse but is more indirect ... i.e. work on the mind, work on the body. When the mind is healthy, it will naturally strive for a healthy body, as one of the desired aims of physical incarnation is a FULL, COMPLETE AND ENJOYABLE LIFE.

It could be said that everyone now living in physical incarnation is existing in a state of complete Bliss or Paradise; it is merely that they are not aware of this fact at a conscious level.

More on mind-body?

The mind-body construct has been PERFECTLY designed for the harvesting of EXPERIENCE in the Physical Plane, but the individual condensed expression of Pure Consciousness is *superior to and in control of both the mind and the body.* This is a paramount "tip" to keep in mind during the daily life experience in the Physical Plane ... I am an Immortal spiritual being and always have been, so what's the BIG DEAL HERE, EH?

Discuss, in a general way, health and health issues.

What one could say regarding "health issues" is that they are ALL IN THE MIND. When the mind is clear and still like an Oriental pond, the health issues vanish like the miasma that they are. There is now, and never has been, any reason at all for the individualized expression of Pure Consciousness that IS a human being to rely on any EXTERNAL means of health "improvement" or solution.

As health deficiencies are *generated and caused by the lower mind,* then one merely does whatever ... therapy, takes whatever substance, utilizes Kriya Yoga, T'ai Chi or what-have-you, and sooner or later all of the problems "leave," as they are not of the Innate SELF-COMPLETE nature.

Speak to the Nei Kung discipline.

(For an examination of the Nei Kung, which comes from the Chinese Amitabha (Amida in Japanese) sect of Buddhism, including instruction in the practice, see **Meditation for Healing** by Justin F. Stone.)

When we consider that there are many different ways to approach the Great Goal, so to speak, we can see that the Nei Kung is one of these many ways that is coming to light during these very interesting times. Although it is true that one can consider the Nei Kung a part of the Buddhist panoply of practice, it can also be said that it is designed in such a way that one may simply, as you know, substitute any phrase desired into the "religion specific" areas and get the same result. We might view this as simply a choice to use different names to describe or access the same place of consciousness or energy.

There is now, and never has been, anything at all to be afraid of or concerned with regarding esoteric practice, it is merely the LACK OF INFORMATION that causes people to fear these simple and wonderful tools. Once again, what can there possibly be to be afraid of in a Sea of Pure Being? Nothing, I think .... "the only thing we have to fear is FEAR ITSELF."

The essence of Pure Consciousness is that it lies BEYOND all concepts of right/wrong, day/night, Yin/Yang, etc. Pure Consciousness is simply Pure Being, so to speak, so what "shoulds" can there possibly be in a Field of Pure, Free Beingness? There is only Joy and Bliss at the miracle of existence and gratitude for the inherent possibilities.

I am not sleeping well and am pretty tired ... commentary?

If we consider that the process of spiritual growth is one of RAPIDLY ACCELERATING UNFOLDMENT, we can see that as this process accelerates, the physical form may, at times, have difficulty "keeping up." This is of no consequence, as these things quickly work themselves out and another level or "plateau" is reached, wherein the individual will stabilize more for a while.

Energetically you are progressing at a rapid pace and this is good .... merely stick with the various practices .... there are many people who back off the practices at this point and, while this is certainly understandable and OK, the *easiest transition through any "energy work" period is achieved by merely continuing with the spiritual practice.*

The entire process can be viewed as one of cleansing and refinement of ALL of the bodies (increasing the vibration), and so we can see that there are times when individuals are more emotional, when disturbing thoughts arise, physical illnesses manifest, etc. Have no concern at all about any of these things as they are temporary. For the most FUN ride through, merely OBSERVE as you let things go that are upsetting, and experience the FREEDOM that is already everyone's NATURAL CONDITION.

Discuss the usefulness of the Orgone blanket.

(The Orgone blanket is one type of "Orgone Accumulator" invented by Wilhelm Reich, a psychiatrist, in the early 20th century. Wilhelm Reich had independently "discovered" the chi, or Vital Force, and called it "Orgone Energy." Please see the information on how to make an Orgone blanket that I have included below.)

The Orgone blanket is a wonderful and easy to make health tool. It is like many things that operate at a "higher" or more Essential level ... IT IS SIMPLE. If a person will merely open up to its usage, it will grant the individual, through time, a much greater level of physical health, as it works with the chi or health energy (second chakra energy). However, here's the problem, Bucko .... not many people will be open to it because they cannot feel energy flow and will not perceive that it is doing anything.

Whether or not they can directly experience the energy flow, it is most assuredly contributing to their personal energy because it is basically an "accumulator" or a device that "draws in" the chi or orgone energy. If individuals would merely give it a try for some time (6 months or greater), they will see results. This, coupled with the fact that it is extremely easy to make and its use is COMPLETELY PASSIVE, makes it a powerful energy tool. You will find that there are many people that have used this device after Wilhelm Reich "discovered" it and made it known ... it is just not known in the culture at large because of its highly esoteric and experimental nature.

Make An Orgone (Chi) Energy Blanket!!

For anyone who is interested in making for themselves a simple and useful tool that has the potential of greatly increasing their level of health and well-being, I would suggest the Orgone energy blanket. It's fun and easy to make. A little background information first.

Many different cultures have understood that there exists in Nature an *Intrinsic Energy* that the Chinese have known about for millennia and call the **Chi**. It exists within and without of all things.

It has been described as the Vital Force or Life Force and is what the Chinese doctors manipulate when they perform acupuncture. In the early 20th Century, a man by the name of *Wilhelm Reich* independently discovered it and called it **Orgone Energy.** He then proceeded to design and manufacture what he called Orgone Accumulators, of which the Orgone blanket is one design.

The Orgone Accumulators of Reich were made in many shapes and sizes, many of a "box type" design, of which the fundamental consideration was a combination or "layering" of organic and inorganic materials. This was merely a direct utilization of the Great Opposites, Yin and Yang, with the inorganic material being the Yang component and the organic being the Yin. As it is the case that everything is basically simple, this type of direct utilization of Yin and Yang is very powerful. To clarify, Yin and Yang can merely be thought of as the **oppositional polarity inherent in vibration** ... and, as we know from science, everything in our world is vibrating. In operation, the Orgone Accumulators work by "drawing in" or accumulating Chi from the surrounding energy environment. The Orgone blanket utilizes a soft organic (usually wool) to "sandwich" an inorganic (steel wool or aluminum foil).

To make one, merely take wool and sandwich between it a layer of aluminum foil. Technically, any organic (like cotton) and metallic inorganic should work fine. I have found the easiest way to make one of a useful size is to merely take a wool sweater and slide "doubled" aluminum foil inside, affixing it with safety pins so that it will stay put and can be changed when the foil becomes damaged. You may then want to remove the arms from the sweater or utilize a sweater-vest for construction instead. This can then be worn on the lap while sitting, causing quite a considerable upflow of energy, easily detectable by some people. If you desire, a larger size can be made from wool blankets by sandwiching a layer of steel wool in-between and sewing as required.

Consistent daily use of the Orgone blanket can bring **substantial health benefits** within some short amount of time. If one likes to read or watch TV, it can easily be worn during these times, as it is completely passive in operation.

Is it true that the Spring and Fall equinoxes are a spiritual time because of the balance of Yin and Yang energies at these times?

Well, what we could say is that these times are wonderful for spiritual practice and progress because of this very fact. If we consider that when Yin and Yang are in balance in the world, this aids the attainment of balance in the individual, and, as we know, this balance allows the Stillness of Consciousness to be revealed in various ways (hence the imposed stillness of meditation). It is true that those that are engaged in spiritual practice are working to "discover" or "self-reveal" the condition of Pure Being that already exists are the core of their Essence, so we can see that any dynamic which occurs in the world at large (e.g. stillness at sunrise and sunset) can assist in this purpose.

Discuss Enlightenment.

DO NOTHING - YOU ARE ALREADY THERE!! This means that one must merely and completely *Be as you would Be.* This means - do what you will at any point in time. To experience life as less than this would be LIMITING, now wouldn't it?

Enlightenment is the complete (or Whole) understanding that *you are "there" now*! You are completely Free to Be as you will and Do as you will, so "do" just that, without holding back. The existence of so many "shoulds" in the various spiritual disciplines has been very detrimental, as it has merely caused people to CONTRACT rather than EXPAND into what they are, as an Innate Essence.

If we consider that these times are ones of expansion, we can see that to contract is sorta "not with the program," so to speak, and is generally to be transcended or avoided. In the Swimming Sea of Consciousness, there are many Condensed Expressions of Pure Consciousness, and these are ALL DESTINED TO REACH THE PLACE THAT THEY ALREADY ARE, at a higher level of Being.

How should "spiritual laws" or "rules" be viewed?

Freedom of the Heart can be described in this way: there is nothing but Love for everything that exists; there is nothing but

COMPLETE AND UTTERLY UNBOUNDED FREEDOM. This is a freedom that is not bound by any spiritual "laws," "rules," or "regulations," which are all limitations of one sort or another. The "laws, rules and regulations" were always meant to be only GUIDELINES! Everyone is FREE NOW, not later! These guidelines were meant to help bring the conscious awareness of human beings back to knowledge of their Innate Nature, by simply reducing internal mental conflicts. Any and all that don't perform this service may be disregarded.

Discuss crystals.

Crystals, being Consciousness, are engaged in a symbiotic relationship with other Beings ... they assist in refining the other Being's vibration, and the use of them by the other Being assists them in refining their consciousness. It is a simple thing, really ... give and get. The use of crystals will, in general, quicken the evolutionary process and allow the individualized essence of consciousness to experience conditions of heightened consciousness during their use, always a fun thang!

Is it true that if one merely engages in Kriya Pranayama, T'ai Chi and other methods of cerebrospinal refinement, one will make rapid progress spiritually without any other kind of intellectual input, like from spiritual teachings?

(Kriya Pranayama is a central practice of Kriya Yoga, which is a guru/chela (teacher/student) method of spiritual development, as are most historic spiritual paths. Its most prominent proponent and well-known guru in the west was Paramahansa Yogananda.)

If we consider that each individualized essence of the All is on a slightly distinct path that will bring them to a wonderful place where they "want" and is natural for them to be, then we can see that the individual must merely FOLLOW HIS BLISS, to use Joseph Campbell's expression, or go to what they are drawn to, OR "EN-JOY" THEMSELVES, or follow their Joy.

In the swimming Sea of Consciousness, there is all the linear time in the world for individual liberation, and it is merely that one can begin helping others more fully when one has attained a certain state of Realization. There is no need to be concerned with "lack" or, to put it another way, the sense that something is being "done wrong" as this merely creates *tension*, which is undesired in spiritual practice. When we consider that everyone will ALWAYS EVENTUALLY GET TO THE PLACE THEY NEED TO BE, we can see that there is plenty of time for "relaxing into" wherever you are at the time.

So, in terms of expansion of consciousness, or cerebrospinal refinement, things just keep getting BETTER AND BETTER?

You got it Bucko! Let me stress here that all that is necessary is merely the application of the various techniques designed to refine the cerebrospinal system ... EVERYTHING ELSE TAKES CARE OF ITSELF. There is no need to follow any "moral" plan or lifestyle, although the conscious selection of these can be helpful and further assist the process. The unfoldment of "morality" or compassion in the individual occurs, as Itzhak Bentov has said, NATURALLY with the refinement of the cerebrospinal system, and so there is literally *nothing else required to progress spiritually at all!*

One does not need to "process" mental and emotional stuff?

As has been said time and time again, it is the CESSATION OF THE MIND STUFF, to reference Patanjali's Yoga Sutras, that enables the "light stuff" to shine right on through!! Now, and I will stress this, the "emotional stuff" can be viewed, like the mind stuff, *as a lower expression of Being.* It is not through "working on it" or "processing it" that one attains, but instead through the realization that YOU ARE NOT YOUR MIND OR EMOTIONS. This is to say that a person can be completely messed up emotionally and still attain the highest realization, because it lies *above the emotions*, vibrationally and energetically.

All of the illumined yogis of all different lands say the same thing ... lack of knowledge of the Spiritual Realms is caused by: over-fixation on things of the Physical Plane and over-involvement with the mental and emotional bodies or components. One can merely RELAX all of the lower bodies, i.e. make them STILL, and see what shines through! My advice will always be, *let go of things that are bothering you, mentally or emotionally.* Let go quick and let go fast, as the consciousness then merely RETURNS TO THAT WHICH IT ALWAYS IS, without the modification of the lower bodies.

How about the implication in some spiritual paths that if things are not being done a certain way that they are being "done wrong"?

There is nothing being "done wrong" for, as you know, everyone merely comes from the place of BEING that they are currently residing in. This is GOOD AND PERFECT, and this is why, especially, one doesn't want to have too many expectations as they merely Self-create their own place of Suffering. EXPECTATION IS LIMITATION!

This means one must merely *enjoy* things the way they are at any point in time or *relax* into things as they are or *groove* with the all. I would say that, in doing this, one laughs a lot more and is more present and flowing with the Tao. This is all there is to it, but, once again, ANY concept should be ignored if it is causing circular mental activity or WORRY, as the lower mind will "get at it" and try to analyze it and apply it to everything or not. This interferes with merely Being, or "grooving," as it were, and should be avoided when possible.

Any more information for me on cerebrospinal refinement?

Do not be concerned with anything at all, if possible, and just laugh a lot ... there can be nothing to be concerned with in a Sea of Pure Bliss and you have had substantial experience to back you up on this! The easiest path through any period of transition is had by merely RELAXING INTO ANY PLACE THAT ONE FINDS ONESELF.

As it is the case that we can view the manifested realms of existence as a Play of Consciousness, we can see that *no experience can ever, in any way, harm the Essential Nature of the human unit of consciousness.* The person that has actualized this realization lives from a place of Freedom because they understand, finally, that they have always been free and continue to remain free now and forever ... this is not something that can be taken away or removed.

If a person is free now and will be free in the future, then the task is merely to learn how to APPRECIATE THIS FREEDOM IN THE WAKING CONSCIOUSNESS ... something that is accomplished very nicely by utilizing the various methods that refine the cerebrospinal system. Doesn't it seem that the easiest thing to do is merely the easiest thing to do ... LIVE IN JOY NOW?

There is never any reason to wait, as you know, for JOY IS NOT DEPENDENT ON ANY EXTERNAL CIRCUMSTANCE, but springs naturally from the Innate Nature. It is merely necessary to remove any tension and blocking processes which, generally, spring from the lower mind ... which is engaged in a dynamic of logical analysis of the things necessary to sustain life and survive. The big problem here is ... there is NOTHING AT ALL NECESSARY TO SURVIVE, ULTIMATELY, because the individualized units of consciousness are Immortal energy beings! This whole "thang" comes from the "kill or be killed" world of the Animal Reality, which is useful at a certain level of evolution and destructive at a certain later point.

Discuss the increasing "energy interface" with the manifested realms during spiritual unfoldment and its practical and other applications.

As an individualized unit of Pure Consciousness gains access to the state or condition which is already his (in higher realms or states of Being) then the energy/consciousness interface with the various worlds will NATURALLY BE GREATER THROUGH LINEAR TIME. This is because of the spiritual unfoldment and is merely the simple nature of the way things work. The individualized unit of consciousness will be able, in greater and greater capacity, to manifest those things that it desires. This will occur either CONSCIOUSLY through the use of visualization and intention, or will occur UNCONSCIOUSLY through the EXACT SAME

METHODS. This is why it is said that one is creating one's own reality.

It is true that as one ascends the ladder of higher energy/consciousness access one will naturally be drawn to those things more suited to their basic nature, though one may still have CULTURAL CONDITIONINGS to overcome. These, of course, include various "shoulds," etc. As one increases and improves their energy interface with the physical surroundings, they are able to utilize, with a certain fullness of time, the various Innate abilities, which of course everyone already has, and these abilities can be used as needed to make one's way in the world. It is the OVER-ATTACHMENT to these things that has been historically warned against.

My right hand is vibrating quite a bit during T'ai Chi, can you explain and illuminate?

As it is the case that you are undergoing a period of intense transformation which is accompanied by intense CLEANSING AND BALANCING, we can say that the unconscious operation of your right hand is merely an expression of the Yang energetic component and the movement is indicative of ongoing balancing operations in your energy bodies. As you might suspect, this is PERFECT for you at this point in time and is nothing to be concerned with. Merely relax into it and allow it to express without tension or restriction as much as possible.

At a certain stage of refined balance, the circumstances and events which will then occur in the Physical Plane of existence (daily life) will exude a similar quality of balance and harmony. You are doing very well with your practice, as some are wont to cease practice for awhile when they experience the tiredness and changes that naturally accompany unfoldment. However, and let me stress this again, *the calmest seas through any period of cleansing and through the whole unfoldment process are attained by merely continuing with the spiritual practice.*

Cessation of practice means continuation of PRESENTLY OCCURRING CIRCUMSTANCES, which would then change or unfold at a greatly reduced rate. This is generally undesired in spiritual practice and unfoldment because it is viewed as a place of continued suffering. The essence of balancing and cleansing is this: these processes are merely the NATURAL REMOVAL OF NEGATIVE (or low vibration) ENERGIES which impede the expression and progress of the Soul.

Comment on "relaxation is the key."

Well, what one could say is that about sums it up! There is no other, greater, easier way to reach a place of more openness than to RELAX AS FULLY AND COMPLETELY AS POSSIBLE into whatever circumstance one might find oneself in. This is truly "the key" as it enables the person who is so inclined to FLOW more into whatever activity or non-activity they are engaged in. It could be said that it is merely the inability to relax and open that is causing so many problems in the human sphere of existence today.

When one relaxes, TENSIONS and stressors that may have been restricting the free flow of energy/consciousness are removed (to one degree or another) and the unit of consciousness will enter into a dynamic of more FLOW, peace, focused concentration and less worry. Worry is the negative "circular" activity of the mind that is concerned with *activities or occurrences that might or might not happen in the future.* If one is living in the NOW then there can be no time for concern about the future except in a direct, focused "planning" sort of way.

WORRY IS NEGATIVE ACTIVITY and should be avoided at all costs .... it is not productive in the least and merely contributes to the pervasively negative collection of thought-forms already in mass consciousness. While we can consider that worry is sometimes very difficult to avoid in your culture, we can see that it serves no practical purpose and does not produce the solution to any problem, REAL OR PERCEIVED.

When we consider that freedom of choice is the inherent nature of the human unit of consciousness, the individual human is always free to choose a place of no worry and greater relaxation, REGARDLESS OF THE CIRCUMSTANCES that the person finds himself in. In doing this, the person will feel more "present," alive, and "flowing in the Now." The events and occurrences that take place in the Physical Plane are merely a Play or Dance of Experience and do not harm the Essential Nature of the human unit of consciousness. It can't be stressed enough that RELAXATION IS TRULY THE KEY to enlarged states of consciousness and greater access to a good life.

While it could be said that one can find a worry-free life through many means, it is always true that one can merely CHOOSE NOT TO WORRY IN ANY CIRCUMSTANCE. Do not worry about money. Do not worry about status. Do not worry about whether or not you are "doing something right" (or wrong). Do not worry about the adventures and explorations to be found in spirituality and expanded consciousness. As we know, there can be nothing to worry about in an Ocean of Pure Being or Consciousness, for there is nothing that is "separate" that could be considered a "threat" or "lack."

What would you say about the practice of keeping a calm, non-reactive perspective no matter what is occurring ... that is, not allowing anything to disturb your consciousness?

What I would say, Mark, is that this is the way of success, both in life and in spiritual practice. There is now, and never has been, ANYTHING to worry about or allow to affect your consciousness in an "upset" or disturbed manner, and this is simply because you, and everyone, are *already at the place you seek* at a higher level of Being. You are already where you are "going," the "goingness" of this process merely makes you CONSCIOUSLY AWARE OF WHAT IS.

The long respected practice of maintaining a Still consciousness in spite of what OCCURS, what you might READ, what you might THINK, or who might insult you or behave in a way that leads to upset, is very good because it simply is a place of greater and greater freedom from fear, the great Constrictor.

There is nothing written in any book that CHANGES ANYTHING from being the way that IT IS NOW and has always been. There is information that is incorrect and misleading and there are perspectives that, although accurate, are really "not for" or "won't be understood by" certain units of consciousness. This is why you merely go toward what you are drawn to, allowing nothing to disturb or disrupt the groovy, smooth, and already still lake of your Consciousness.

What is the key to "flowing" with these changing times?

Merely BE THAT WHICH YOU ARE NOW!! This is the secret and the key, there is NO OTHER. Every condensed expression of Pure Consciousness must merely Be as they will Be, as this will eventually, after much kicking and screaming, bring them around to the place that they ALREADY LOVE ... or to put it another way, the things that they already don't love merely leave!! What would be the sense in anything less than this? This is not some CONTROL-O-THON HERE, BUCKO!! It could best be said that the individualized expression will eventually figure out that they are headed to a place of "Moreness" where they like and want to be now!

Any more thoughts on the Pure Joy of Being?

If we consider that there is NOTHING AT ALL BUT PURE JOY, ANYWHERE, then we can begin to see that many of the mental and emotional obscurations of the realization of Pure Joyousness can be characterized as generated by the *sole instrument of the lower mind.* The lower mind is LIMITED in its ability to understand or grasp things that are subjective or intuitive in nature. As it is limited, it cannot conceptualize in any adequate way THE UNLIMITED.

As it is the case that many people in your realm consider that the only way to survive and gain HAPPINESS is through *struggle and strife or competition,* which is behavior that can be viewed as directly oppositional to the type of "relaxed Beingness" required to access the Oceans and Oceans of Joy that EXIST EVERYWHERE RIGHT NOW, it could be said that the road to Joyousness is a hard and difficult battle for some in its EASY SIMPLICITY. There is certainly no need, and never has been, for the amount of goofiness, anger, struggle, mean-spirited competition, etc. that has gone on and continues to occur in your realm. It is merely *ignorance* that keeps people locked in the chains of competition. In a Sea of Pure Dancing

Joy, what need is there for any competition when there is ABUNDANCE FOR ALL?

Before we examine the next section of channeled material, I want to take a moment to address the use of symbols in spiritual work. Symbols are used in Reiki and other systems to access various energies or levels of consciousness and this is because at a certain level of consciousness transference of information takes place through the use of symbols. The Antahkarana symbol is not a "Reiki" symbol, but is known in the Reiki community, as it is associated with Tibetan Buddhism. There is a strong connection between Reiki and Tibetan Buddhism, regardless of any "historical origin" relationships. This symbol is very powerful and merely being in its presence is said to activate or stimulate the connection between the High Self and the lower "bodies" or vehicles of consciousness. I have personally found that it definitely effects the energetic system and is useful and so I reproduce it below.

Discuss and describe the Antahkarana symbol and its usage.

If we consider that this symbol is a very ancient means of interconnecting the various aspects (bodies) of the individualized unit of Pure Consciousness, we can see that it is an extremely powerful and simple tool. While it is true that it has remained largely unknown down through the ages, it is now time, as it is time with other esoteric information, for these things to become more widely known. You are familiar with this symbol from past life experiences as a Tibetan Buddhist, where it is employed as a focus of meditation and a "good omen" symbol.

If we consider that many such tools as this will be necessary during these very interesting and different times, we can understand that this is why they are naturally coming forth. This symbol is very powerful and should be utilized daily ... it works to integrate the High Self with the personality self. This symbol, being of the higher realms of consciousness, IS SIMPLE, is it not? It is powerful and works to help further the whole-self integration process, always a process of EXPANSION OR "MORENESS."

I think you will find that, as you relax into things more and more, as you are basically wont to do, that things work out wonderfully in a way that I can only say will be like the visions of the Green Place ... just ALIVE AND GROOVY ... Freedom and Pure Love. There is, quite simply, nothing to be concerned with and this will be apparent once a certain level of consciousness has been attained (i.e. - looking back).

This symbol has its roots in the Sky and its history with the Tibetan Buddhists ... once again, it is a wonderful, SIMPLE, interconnecting tool. The symbol itself, in any of its various drawings, is like other symbols that you are familiar with ... it basically IS consciousness, and as such, one must merely be in its presence, like any other Being, in order to reap energy benefits. I realize that this will be difficult to grasp from the perspective of the Physical Plane, but every day you learn to let go intellectually of things that can't be intellectually grasped and just enjoy them, silly, just enjoy them!! These things are aspects of consciousness, and concepts can be helpful, but as John Selby has said, they can also hold us back or drag us down in our explorations. Now we wouldn't want THAT, would we?

I am tired and obviously going through "cleansing" symptoms ... discuss and describe.

As you know, the cleansing of the various vehicles of consciousness is a NATURAL process which results in a fuller expression of the Innate "Being-Nature" of the individual. During this process, there are periods where the following symptoms will manifest: unusual tiredness, "flu-like" feelings due to the cleansing of the upper chakras, dehydration requiring the INGESTION OF LOTS 'O WATER!, various emotional and mental states that are reflective of the polar nature of your reality ... i.e. one minute up, one down, etc.

It might be said that all of these symptoms are there to be WELCOMED, because they are short-term and allow for greater innate happiness, contentment, satisfaction, knowledge of purpose, and experience of the Divine Qualities including Bliss, Love, Peace, Joy, Truth, etc. In a swimming Sea of Consciousness, there is nothing to be concerned with regarding these types of transitory cleansings and they should merely be endured in one manner or another. Here are some suggestions to ease the transition: WATER, WATER, WATER ... SPIRITUAL PRACTICE, AND RELAXATION WHENEVER POSSIBLE. These things will all work out leaving you swimming in a sea of Bliss!!

More on this tiredness caused by cleansing?

As it is the case that, once again, your various vehicles of consciousness are being refined for the greater expression of your Being Nature, you might expect that you will have to endure "the sufferings," as this period is known, wherein negative energies are being released from the individualized consciousness. THIS IS A BENEFICENT PROCESS! Do not be concerned in the least during this time with various mental and emotional things as they are merely in the process of release from the consciousness.

Please merely relax into whatever place you find yourself .... it is unnecessary to engage in mental speculation regarding ANY ASPECT OF THIS PROCESS, especially if that speculation generates increased tension or concern. There is nothing to be concerned about; this is a beneficent process which is a place of "MORENESS" and not a diminished place or a place of lack or pain.

It is common for the individual to feel that they are "losing control" or "losing themselves" or "losing their mind" or "losing whatever," but in reality they are *gaining aspects of themselves consciously that already exist at a higher level of Being,* which you are well aware of and have a fairly comprehensive and complete grasp of, to the degree that an intellectual grasp can be had of this type of thing. Over-conceptualization is LIMITATION!!

This is the thing that is impossible to completely convey ... everyone is going to a place of NO LIMITS, which is inherently beyond conceptualization. You would do well at times to merely *observe as you relax into various circumstances.* Human units of consciousness are IMMORTAL CONDENSATIONS OF PURE CONSCIOUSNESS and the different systems of philosophy/religion have adopted various ways of conceptualizing this, some of which are helpful and some of which are guaranteed to generate more fear, an undesired circumstance in spiritual growth.

So, during spiritual unfoldment, ALL of the various bodies or vehicles of consciousness are refined ... this should effect the person's experience in ANY realm that they find themselves in ... commentary?

If we consider that everyone is currently undergoing refinement of consciousness, some more quickly than others due to level of spiritual practice and previous condition of development/evolution, we can see that each individualized expression of Pure Consciousness is reaching for the stars a little at a time. What this means is that generally, the refinement of the various bodies occurs in this manner: the "higher" bodies undergo refinement first and then these effects and "changes," or more technically, UNFOLDMENTS, filter down through the various bodies, much in the manner that electricity is "stepped down" in a step-down transformer.

This process results in the individualized essence of consciousness being able to more fully experience that which it already is, at a higher level of Being. It is the case that refinement of the cerebrospinal system through the accumulation and utilization of the chi or psychic energy is the mechanism for the refinement of all of the bodies while in physical incarnation. And it is true that the evolution of the bodies (increasing the vibration) brings about a PERMANENT CHANGE IN THE OVERALL "MANIFESTED" EXPERIENCE, i.e. the individual finds himself in progressively better and better (more and more Innate) circumstances in whichever realm he is currently occupying. There is no more sure path to accelerated spiritual growth than the various methods of "energy work" which all quickly work to refine the cerebrospinal system.

As life is Everlasting, and cannot be taken away, then we are merely engaged in various experiences, whether in the physical or any other realm ... commentary?

Well, Mark, I would say that you've got a handle on this baby!! Yes!! It's simple, really. Every individualized unit of Pure Consciousness has ALWAYS existed and WILL ALWAYS EXIST, so the problem is, you see, not that which is commonly perceived in your realm - one of Life and Death, but MERELY ONE OF FASTER OR SLOWER GROWTH!! There is, quite simply, no other process going on in the manifested worlds, as this is their sole purpose. "The manifested realms exist for the use and growth of the Soul," or something like that from Patanjali's Yoga Sutras (II-21).

You will find that life will get easier and easier as you merely do as you're inclined to do and RELAX INTO THAT SUCKER!! If we can conceive that all of the things that are occurring in the Physical Plane of existence are taking place merely as a Grand Dance of Consciousness, then we can see that, once again, no one is being harmed by these experiences, as you know; they are merely having them in physical incarnation or in some other realm or form. The essence of everything is SIMPLICITY ... there is no "essential complexity" as all complexity springs from simplicity.

Roy's creative imagination technique looks pretty good ... commentary?

(This refers to Roy Eugene Davis, a chela or disciple of Yogananda and the head of the Center for Spiritual Awareness.)

As it is the case that the reality of the Physical Plane of existence is each day being created and maintained by the combined thought-forms of those humans in physical incarnation, we can see that the consistent application of "mind science" will enable the individualized unit of Pure Consciousness to *change the physical circumstances and situations in which they find themselves.*

Although it is the case that only the very few utilize the technique, it is very powerful and will enable the person to rapidly attain certain desired goals and/or ends. This is, of course, what you and I have already discussed, merely synthesized and formed into a neat procedure for people to use .... it all boils down to INTENTION and DESIRE coupled with IMAGINATION (visualization).

Roy utilizes the wonderful term "Mind Substance" to describe the sea of unformed Reality in which inhabitants of the Physical Plane are swimming. Since the human mind is merely a HIGHER VIBRATIONAL EXPRESSION OF CONSCIOUSNESS than the elements or things of the Physical Reality, then *consciously or unconsciously,* it is busily going about manufacturing our daily reality for us. The use of this procedure will assist the person in gradually changing the contents of the subconscious mind, which, as Roy says, will merely accept any objective or firmly implanted subjective experience as a new "reality template."

How are results manifested during the process of visualization?

It is the case that you are engaged in a process of learning how to directly manifest, through the processes of visualization and intention, those things that you desire at any point in time, and, as this unfolds more in you, things will merely COME TO YOU ... YOU DO NOT HAVE TO SEEK THEM OUT.

If we conceptualize the essence of the Physical Plane as one of *experience*, then we can see that the individualized condensations of Pure Consciousness are each going about finding the ways and manners that *are suited to them in terms of harvesting experience.* You will not find that many people, in these times, will have much success with sticking with things that are not within their own personal range of FLOW.

Speak to the use of synchronized breathing in T'ai Chi and other movement disciplines.

The classic breathing techniques of various cultures, and especially those associated with Yoga, are of a nature that merely enables one to access and utilize more prana/chi than one would without them. If we consider that a "fuller breath" will provide MORE OVERALL CHI but will also provide a "more grounded" or rooted experience, we can see why some will prefer the more refined, naturally occurring breathing, as they prefer the experiences inherent in this more refined state (expanded consciousness, seeing more of the perfection in everything, and others).

The experiences are wonderful, but, as you know, in the end it is the operative evolutionary mechanisms (read chi/prana/kundalini) that REFINE THE CEREBROSPINAL SYSTEM AND CRACK THE NUT, so to speak. I would suggest that it would be useful to employ a little of both experiences ... sometimes the "fuller breath," sometimes the "natural breath." I will stress this again, *it is the utilization and accumulation of chi/prana that is the operative mechanism of unfoldment/evolution.*

More information on the wonderful Antahkarana symbol?

This symbol is the essence of SIMPLICITY, is it not? And yet it is very powerful, yes? This alone is a great secret that kings and princes have struggled to comprehend through the ages ... EVERYTHING TRULY POWERFUL IS VERY SIMPLE. This symbol is an incredible secret, worth lots of earthly treasure, because by its passive use alone it rapidly hastens the individual unfoldment and integration. You will find that daily use is the way of progress!!

If we conceptualize this symbol as representative of the connection between the High Self and the lower vehicles or bodies, we can see that its usage will speedily increase the firmness and completeness of this connection. It is a wonderful tool and can be used by all to great benefit, although of course some will not perceive energy flows or any sign that it is "doing anything."

In the swimming sea of Consciousness, there are many, many tools which are becoming available at this point in history, as you know. If these are "tested" and found useful, they are there for the further progress of individuals such as yourself, who will "experiment" or take the risk involved in using them. MANY WILL NOT, and so encouragement and support are groovy things, maybe causing one who would not use these things to give them a try. When it becomes apparent to the individual through, of course, *their own usage* that these things are valuable, then they will be utilized.

Once again last night I saw symbols or patterns in my sleep ... what do these mean and what information, if any, is being transmitted?

The essence of the patterns is one of simplicity ... they transfer certain "information" which is also analogous to the transfer of consciousness. As has been discussed, the symbolic form of communication is utilized in the higher realms and is merely another method of transfer of consciousness, MORE REFINED THAN VERBAL COMMUNICATION. Since everyone in incarnation is existing on different levels or planes simultaneously, a certain part of your being understands these symbols and can utilize them.

Have no concern about this process, it is merely the way things work and is occurring in every single incarnate human. On a higher level than the symbol/pattern talk exists DIRECT CONSCIOUSNESS TRANSFER, also referred to as "light-talk." This is very subtle and sublime and this ability merely unfolds with time and further spiritual practice, as it is another result of cerebrospinal refinement.

Some Spiritual Practices

There is a wide variety of spiritual practices known in every society and culture of the world, and I wanted to share with the reader some of the methods that I use and have found very helpful.

Consistent application of the more powerful of these practices will bring results - spiritual practices are *scientific* in nature. This means if one will merely utilize the methods that they are drawn to, preferably **daily** whenever possible, they *will* see results and progressive unfoldment of consciousness. Many of the practices that come from various types of yoga have been found "tried and true" by countless numbers of aspirants. Like achieving results from physical exercise or dieting, *consistent application of the practice is what is required.* This can't be over-emphasized. What we are attempting to do with sadhana is to allow the innermost consciousness-essence to blossom into the waking or "daily" consciousness of the individual. Once again, this is an **already extant state**, it merely requires conscious Realization.

One of the major ways that we assist the process of consciousness expansion is by opening the various chakras and by increasing the flow of prana (or life-force) through the physical body. Disease in humans is caused primarily by restrictions or blockages occurring in what the Chinese call the various meridians and channels of Chi flow, which are merely the pathways along which the life energy naturally travels. In our culture, *stress and tension* are the main factors contributing to these blockages, and so **relaxation** is the simple antidote to restore vibrant health, along with some "body work" and physical exercise. There are also techniques to directly stimulate prana flow in the meridians and channels, which are useful.

I will be recommending a wide spectrum of practices here, including kundalini yoga, and I want to stress that *none of these practices can harm you in the least*. Some of them may lead to some very intense and unusual experiences, but extremes can easily be avoided in any endeavor. Contemplate the fact that you are **now**, not later, an Immortal spiritual being and not a body or mind and you will see the impossibility of anything harming you. In my opinion, steady, consistent application of the techniques is the way of progress and growth.

Yoga and T'ai Chi

As mentioned above, the tried and true methods that come from the East are to be highly recommended. For the most benefit and progress to be obtained in these practices, it is best to have personal instruction by a knowledgeable person. This is especially true in all forms of T'ai Chi and Chi Kung, as well as Hatha Yoga. One *can* learn the forms from a videotape, however constructive criticism is then not available and is very helpful. I highly recommend the practice of T'ai Chi and Chi Kung, and there are many forms available these days. These would include T'ai Chi Ch'uan of various styles, shorter forms like T'ai Chi Chih, and countless other Chi Kung variations of dynamic (moving) and stationary (e.g. Zhan Zhuang) styles. T'ai Chi and Chi Kung practice is very good for mobilizing the Chi and circulating and balancing it, opening the meridians and channels in the process.

There are many Hatha Yoga instructors in every city and personalized instruction is highly desirable. However, one can learn many of the useful poses from a well done book, such as **The American Yoga Association's Beginner's Manual** by Alice Christensen. The Sun Salutation is a very useful and easy-to-learn sequence which flexes and stretches the spine nicely, very helpful for releasing trapped energies. Additionally, there is a specific "spinal energy set" that comes from kundalini yoga and concludes with the highly useful Sat Kriya that I utilize and suggest for anyone. See **Breathing Methods for Health and Harmony** by Steven Ridley for a simple and usable photographic explanation.

I also highly recommend the practice of the Hatha Yoga posture Savasana, or the Corpse Pose, as a facilitator to relaxation and gradually increasing internal stillness. It is an extremely simple posture: merely lie on your back on the floor, feet spread comfortably apart, toes turned out, palms turned up. Remain still in this posture for *at least* twenty minutes and up to an hour and a half (or longer, if desired). Relax yourself completely, allowing yourself to "melt into" the floor. This will release muscular tensions that may have been restricting the free flow of energy. If you experience pain in any area, unless you have skeletal problems, merely "ride it out" - it will leave when muscular relaxation occurs, releasing trapped energies. Additionally, since body and mind are one, as the body *remains* still the mind *becomes* still. Internal stillness is the desirable state in spiritual practice. "Suffering is of the mind," said the Buddha, and he was right - so still the mind and suffering leaves.

At the risk of greatly upsetting large groups of people, I am going to state that kundalini yoga can be self-taught with good result, as this has been my personal experience. However, if one desires, there are many closely similar systems of kundalini yoga (I am a Kriya Yoga initiate) with which you can become formally allied, and I recommend this as a "best case" scenario. There are certain practices that come from these yogas, previously completely unknown to the larger populace, that one can access only by becoming formally affiliated. That being said, there are many, many excellent books that will enable the serious practitioner to experience the benefits of this powerful yogic tradition. I recommend **Kundalini Awakening** by John Selby, an excellent book which constitutes a complete program and includes a powerful series of yantras (the visual mantra). This is a life-changing book, as is the practice of kundalini yoga.

The Microcosmic Orbit

From Taoist Yoga comes the wonderful practice of the Microcosmic Orbit, which circulates life energy through the two main vertical channels of the body. This practice is similar to kundalini yoga, however kundalini yoga focuses only on the spine (called the "governing channel" by the Chinese) and this practice includes the front channel also (the "functional channel").

To practice the Microcosmic Orbit, seat yourself in any comfortable position so that the spine is held in an erect, upright manner. Place the tongue against the palate or roof of the mouth as far back as comfortable, preferably about half-way back. This facilitates the energetic connection between the two channels. Focus your concentration on the second chakra, called the Tan T'ien (pronounced "dantienne") by the Chinese. This is located just below the navel, about two inches or so. Now, on an in-breath, draw the chi current (which can be visualized as light or a ball of light) from the Tan T'ien through the legs and up the spine to the crown of the head. Gently retain the breath here for a moment. Then, on an out-breath, allow the chi current to descend down the front of the body (like cascading water or light) until it rests again at the Tan T'ien. Focus the concentration here for a moment. Then, begin again.

Repeat this for a number of breaths. After the last circuit, merely rest the concentration for awhile at the Tan T'ien as you breath normally. This is a very powerful practice, which will eventually result in the chi circulating in this circuit by itself naturally, as it does in the human fetus.

Pranayama and Breath Methods

There are many classic breathing techniques that come from yoga and these are known as *pranayama* (translates roughly as "control of the life-force"). I have separated them out so that I might include them with breath work in general, of which there are many practices from different cultures.

When we breathe, we inhale not only oxygen, well known to Western science, but also Prana (or Chi), the life energy - not so well known. Our states of consciousness during the day are reflected by our breath-pattern and form a reciprocal relationship with it. Short, rapid breathing is an obvious sign of unease of some sort and is indicative of some degree of mental turbulence. Since breath-pattern determines the quality and quantity of prana circulating internally, and our quality and quantity of prana forms a reciprocal relationship with our state of mind, if we notice that we are mentally upset, we can *consciously alter our breathing pattern to bring about a calm mental state*.

Try this - breathe in and out softly and normally but hold or pause the breath after the exhale and before the next inhale. Merely hold it for a bit, as long as feels comfortable. Do this for ten minutes or so and notice the calm that descends around you. This technique can be employed if one is upset or concerned about something to bring about a state of greater mental calm.

Because of the relationship between prana, mind, and breath, by the practice of certain breath techniques we can induce desired states of consciousness. We can also bring about conditions of energetic balance and increase accumulations of prana in the system, desirable from an evolutionary perspective. Here are some highly recommended techniques:

Alternate Nostril Breathing

There are three major etheric channels that are associated with the physical spine in human beings. These are ida, pingala, and sushumna channels or nadis. This technique balances the energetic flows in the two polar nadis, ida and pingala, so pranic flows (kundalini) can be encouraged or induced in the central sushumna nadi. It is very simple and requires daily practice to be effective.

Seat yourself comfortably with the spine straight. We are going to breathe in through one nostril and then breathe out through the other one. It doesn't matter which one we begin with. To facilitate this, we will use the thumb and index finger of the right hand to "close off" the nostril we do not wish to breathe through. Bring your right hand up to your nose and use your thumb to close off the right nostril. Breathe in through your left. Release the thumb from the right nostril and close off the left nostril with the index finger. Breathe out through the right nostril. Now, breathe *in* through the right nostril and then "switch" the fingers and breathe out through the left. This is one cycle. This whole process can also be conceptualized as "switching nostrils at the top of the inhale," for this is really all we do. We breathe in through one, switch, breathe out through the other and then breathe back in through the same one, switching only at the top of the inhale.

This practice will cleanse the ida and pingala nadis and balance energy flows between them. It is very good as a preparatory practice for meditation and contributes to a balanced state of mind.

Circular or Connected Breathing

This is a practice that comes from Rebirthing, founded by Leonard Orr. It is a "western pranayama" and is very powerful as it infuses large volumes of prana quickly into the system. The practice of circular breathing, for any length of time, will *definitely* provide the practitioner with experiences of his energetic system.

In some quarters, circular breathing is considered to be an "extreme" practice, but this is nonsense - *this is a very beneficial practice that is not harmful in the least.* Once again, we are **spiritual beings now enjoying a physical experience.** I have found this practice to be stimulating, energizing, and a facilitator to the release of various tensions or trapped energies. It is sometimes helpful, but not necessary, to have a "breath coach" to ensure that you do not "drift off" and discontinue the practice due to wandering concentration.

The practice of circular breathing is extremely, deceptively simple. All you do is connect the inhale and exhale ... that is, there is no pause between the in-breath and the out-breath, as there is in normal breath-patterns. The breath becomes continuous. Breathe at a moderately rapid pace, but not so fast as to hyperventilate. Breathe utilizing the diaphragm, or from what the Chinese call the Tan T'ien (pronounced: "dantienne"). This is equivalent to the second chakra in the Indian metaphysical system and is in the lower abdomen, about two inches below the navel. When you are properly utilizing diaphragmatic breathing, the lower abdomen moves out on inhale and in on exhale. This "belly breathing" is the natural method of breathing for humans (watch a baby or infant) and is only abandoned for tension-creating "chest breathing" as we age.

When using the circular breathing technique, you really only "work" on the in-breath, on the out-breath you merely let the air "fall out" through the natural relaxation of the various muscles utilized in breathing. Find a comfortable rhythm and just go with it. You will find that concentration is necessary as, without it, the breathing will tend to revert to some variation of the normal pattern.

This practice generates large inflows of prana and is *very* helpful in speeding the unfoldment of the innate spiritual potential. Of course, different practitioners will have different experiences, with some people experiencing intense emotional releases and others experiencing release at an energetic level, with little or no conscious involvement.

For an excellent further examination of this powerful practice, see **Breathing Methods for Health and Harmony** by Steven Ridley.

Mantra and Yantra Usage

Perhaps there is no more important and fundamental spiritual practice than the use of mantras and yantras (the visual mantra). A mantra is a specific word or sound which has a certain vibrational or energetic essence. The repetition of these words, aloud or silently, puts one in contact with the consciousness-energy represented by the mantra. Silent repetition of a mantra is very helpful in "taking one beyond" and stilling the mind, thus mantras are often utilized in meditation (more on that below), but can also be chanted aloud for their vibrational potency.

There are countless mantras and yantras that can be utilized. To locate some yantras, you may have to do a little research at the library, although the book **Kundalini Awakening** by John Selby has included within it a set of seven that are vibrationally specific for the seven main chakras and are very powerful and useful. Here are some mantras that I have found personally useful. Choose whichever you are drawn to and then chant them daily. Pronunciation, generally, is pretty much like it appears, but ask someone knowledgeable, if you'd like.

Om

Here it is, the Fundamental Vibration. Chanting Om is highly recommended because Pure Consciousness employs it to manifest the phenomenal realms. Since everything can be reduced back to this fundamental vibration, why not start by utilizing it and see where it leads?

Om Namah Shivaya

This mantra is well known and utilized in various systems of yoga (Kriya and Siddha Yoga, etc.) and has great vibrational potency. Translates roughly as "I salute Shiva, my inner Self."

Om Mani Padme Hum

From Buddhism we have another bone-rattler. Will definitely get all the juices flowing, so to speak. Translates roughly as "Hail to he who is the jewel in the heart of the lotus!" Tibetan Buddhists pronounce this "Om Mahni Pay-may Hung," which I utilize and have found very powerful.

Om Shanti, Shanti, Shanti

This is the great "peace" mantra (Shanti means "peace"). It will bring about a placid and yet quietly joyous state. Very well known. Chant it daily.

Hari Om

This mantra works on the third chakra to gradually cleanse and eliminate fears. Hari is one of the names of Vishnu, the Preserver.

Sat Nam

One of the mantras from kundalini yoga, it has great power. Its meaning is roughly "True Identity." It is pronounced to rhyme with "but, mom!" Utilized in the performance of Sat Kriya.

Hamsa

Also spelled as *Hong-sau* and pronounced "Hong saw." Based on the sound of the in-breath ("Hong") and the out-breath ("saw"). Utilized often as a mental focus in meditation. Translates roughly as "I am That" or "I am He."

So'Ham

The reverse pronunciation of the above mantra.

Namu Amida Butsu

This is the Nembutsu, which comes from the Pure Land sect of Buddhism associated with the Amida (Amitabha) Buddha, the Buddha of Infinite Light. Very nice high vibration.

Ah

This mantra or sound is known is various traditions, including Sufism and Tibetan Buddhism. It is a *very* powerful, expansive, heart chakra opening mantra. Chant it daily. See Steven Ridley's **Breathing Methods** book mentioned above for a detailed practice using the breath with this mantra.

Eeeeee

This sound resonates with the crown chakra and is very useful.

Mmmm

This sound resonates with the "third eye" or brow chakra. Made like the sound of buzzing bees.

There are, of course, many more mantras which you can discover by studying yoga, Hinduism, Buddhism, and other traditions. Try 'em out and sense the vibratory component to see if they are useful for you.

A practice that I recommend that uses two of the above mantra-sounds is to seat yourself in any comfortable position, then breathe in through your heart chakra and then out through your brow chakra. As you breathe out through the brow chakra, chant "*Mmmmmm.*" Then merely reverse this - breathe in through the brow chakra and out through the heart chakra. As you breathe out through the heart chakra, chant "*Ahhhhh.*" This is a very powerful practice for interconnecting the heart and brow chakras and assisting in opening the spinal nadis.

Mantra usage is a very potent and fun tool. As mentioned earlier, merely "try out" a few of the mantras and stick with the ones that you have an affinity for. Daily chanting, or chanting on most days, is the way of optimal results.

Meditation - Just Sitting and Enjoying the Stillness

Much has been said and written about the practice of meditation. Basically, meditation practice is merely *actively resting in the Essential Being Nature*, to whatever degree. Meditation is not an activity of striving, it is **aware witnessing in Stillness**. This witnessing can be done with eyes open or closed, with or without objects. The fundamental aspect of the practice is the *witnessing*. This means merely observe what is occurring, dispassionately.

Traditional meditation practice involves assuming a *still* and comfortable physical posture, an upright chair is fine unless you are used to, and *comfortable with,* sitting in one of the "cross-legged" positions. Since we are trying to experience the Being Nature, which lies above or "beyond" the level of mind and emotions, we can employ techniques at first to assist us in quieting the mind by giving it something to do. The primary ways to do this include utilizing a mantra and watching the breath.

To perform a "breath watching" type of practice, seat yourself comfortably with spine straight. You may also lie on the floor in the Savasana posture described above, if you are not prone to falling asleep in this type of posture. Close your eyes and become as internally still as possible. Then, without any attempt to control or modify the breath, merely observe or watch it as you naturally inhale and exhale. Watch the whole process, including the natural pauses or spaces between the inhale and exhale. Attempt to become completely absorbed in this process, which will lead one into a place of reduced (to no) thought. If you come to a very still place of Being through the use of this, merely let go of the technique, it has served its purpose, and rest in the stillness of Being.

Use of a mantra is helpful, and has the added impact of inherent vibratory potency. Of the mantras listed above, some of the popular ones to use in this way are *Sat Nam* and *Hong-sau* or *so'ham.* The mantra is repeated silently (mentally) and is synchronized with the natural occurrence of the breath. So, after getting comfortable in a seated position and becoming still, merely choose one of these mantras and then, on an in-breath, silently repeat the first half of the mantra (e.g. "*Sat*"). On the out-breath, repeat the second half of the mantra (e.g. "*Nam*"). As in watching the breath, become completely absorbed in this process until it is naturally transcended into the place of still Beingness. Utilization of "breath-watching" and mantra is **technique**; actively resting and *witnessing* in the place of Still Beingness, to whatever degree, is meditation.

One can easily enjoy the stillness with eyes open, too. Seat yourself in a comfortable position in a quiet and still room and then merely **observe**. Closely inspect the objects in the room. If a dog barks, listen. If there is a clock ticking, listen for as long as the attention is held. This technique, which is also called "being present" or "being here now" leads one into a place of open-eyed meditation, in which very few thoughts occur and you are merely *aware*.

This is a very fun practice once the individual actually tries it for him or herself and comes to the realization that *silence and stillness are not what they might have previously thought!* Most people will not actively plunge into Stillness, but once this is done, it is seen that this is the resting place of Joy and Love.

Meditation practice is very, very valuable and one can easily find more in-depth explorations than this short one. Once again, it is a highly individual practice, so employ the guidelines to help you in getting to the place of Still Beingness and then rest there. *Witnessing as you actively rest in Still Beingness, to whatever degree, is experience of our Being Nature, or meditation.* Some people will require very little use of any technique for meditation practice, and others require more usage. Technique is only used to take you to the stillest place, in any given meditation session.

"Bliss is Everywhere Now" Technique

In the great monistic tradition of Kasmir Shaivism (worship of Shiva or God), there is a practice which is termed the "sadhana of Shiva" in which one merely attempts to affirm that there is only "One Thing," God or Shiva, in a direct and personal way. You would say, "I am God. God is me. Since I am *already* God, I will realize this easily! Everyone and everything I see is God. All is Consciousness, there is no separation anywhere, and that's all there is!" Now this is a very useful practice, although it is somewhat dry. It is an attempt to help us to realize what the already extant nature of Reality is.

To liven it up a bit, first understand that everything is manifested from the Source through the use of the Om vibration. The highest experienced aspect of this vibration is **Bliss**. As mentioned earlier in the channeled information, Bliss is what we and all things *essentially are.* So, merely imagine that everything around you is what it *truly* is: **condensed or frozen Bliss!** Imagine, or feel, that you are Bliss also. You can substitute Love or Joy for Bliss, if you desire. So merely look around and affirm: "It's all solidified Love!! I am swimming in a Sea of Love! Why would I look for Love? *I and everything around me IS ALREADY LOVE!*" This is a very fun and relaxing technique. What is there to fear in an Ocean of Bliss?

Radiate Light and Love from the Heart

This technique is very simple and powerful. All you do is to seat yourself in any comfortable position, on a couch, chair or the floor, and intentionally *visualize* that you are radiating Light and/or Love from the heart chakra in the center of the chest. You can either visualize a constant stream of Light flowing toward some object in the room, or merely radiate Light in all directions, as if there were a star of pure white light located at the heart chakra. In order for this technique to have effect, you must gently concentrate *continually* on this visualization for some period of time, ten minutes or more seems to work for me. You will notice increased energy at this center as your intentional visualization generates outward flow from the center.

Use of Crystals

It has been known for millennia that crystals can be utilized to assist in the expansion of consciousness. As everything is Consciousness, all things are possessed of certain vibratory rates, and in the case of crystals, their potent vibrations can be easily employed in spiritual practice. There are a wide variety of crystal types, all of which have certain applications, and I would refer the reader to any one of a number of general crystal books for more in-depth information. However, I will speak to a few crystal types that are especially useful.

Quartz

This is your general use, all-purpose crystal. Clear quartz crystals are very powerful, with many uses, some of which probably exceed our current ability to functionally grasp, although we may have had this knowledge in the distant past. Quartz crystals can be thought of as reflectors or "focusers" of high vibrational energy. They are morphologically hexagonal, or six-sided. They *terminate* in a point, and two general types are routinely used - **single terminated** and **double terminated**. Energy flows through a single terminated crystal in the direction of the point ... that is, entering at the base and flowing out the point. Double terminated crystals are *bi-directional*, this means that energy flows through the crystal and out of both points, longitudinally. Thus they have differing esoteric applications.

Single terminated crystals can be utilized to direct energy in certain desired ways, creating directional flow. So, they can stimulate flow in the major channels of the body, in whatever direction is desired by the practitioner. They can also create fields of energy in which the practitioner can immerse him or herself. Below is a highly useful crystal layout that is good for opening the heart chakra and excellent as a tool for meditative stillness.

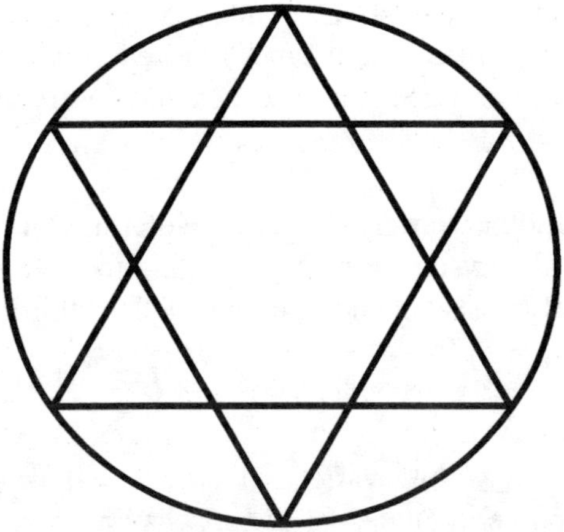

Star of David Crystal Layout

To utilize this layout, one merely places single terminated crystals, points facing in toward the center, at the "points" of the star. Notice that not only does this form a Star of David, but a *circle*. The most powerful layout will include this circular component, that is, it will not be elongated in one direction or another. Notice also that there are two equilateral triangles that are a part of this layout, one pointing up, one down. This is symbolic of the two great components of any polar, vibratory reality - Earth and Sky energy or Shakti and Shiva. Quartz crystals can also be laid out in *triangular* shapes, and will create different energetic flows depending on which direction one faces while within the structure of the triangle.

Merely seat yourself, either in a chair or cross-legged on the floor, in the center of this layout. As I mentioned, this layout generates a field that is conducive to the opening of the heart chakra and very nice for encouraging internal stillness for meditation.

For an excellent, detailed examination on the use of quartz crystals, which includes the above Star of David layout, see **The Complete Crystal Guidebook** by Uma Silbey.

Rose Quartz

There are many different varieties of quartz possessing color. Rose quartz is excellent for the heart chakra and use of it helps to encourage a calm, placid state of mind and being. It is readily available in tumbled pieces, and can be placed over the heart chakra in a layout, or worn as a pendant over the heart. Very useful.

Amethyst

This is another variety of quartz, violet in color. Amethyst is good as a "mental" crystal; it is very soothing to the nervous system. It also can greatly assist in the opening of the "third eye" or brow chakra.

Citrine

Citrine is a yellow variety of quartz that is very good for opening and empowering the solar plexus chakra (third). It focuses a golden, sun-like energy - the essence of active power. Our culture has much to release at this energy center, and the higher aspect of this chakra, which is merely pure, usable, sun-like *power*, needs to be brought forth to empower the higher chakras. Citrine and Danburite, mentioned below, are very helpful in this process.

Albite or Moonstone

Moonstone is the "gemstone" or finished version of albite, which is plagioclase feldspar. Use of either of these versions brings about a calm, placid state as they are very "Yin" energetically. Very soothing. Good stone to be used by those under stresses of any kind, especially mental.

Calcite

Calcite is a very good crystal as it assists in the release of mental concepts that can cause constriction and fear and interfere with spiritual growth. As the lower mind is often the biggest stumbling block in spiritual growth, calcite can greatly assist during transitional times.

Fluorite

Another good "mental" stone, it aids and intensifies the connection between the intuitive or spiritual essence and the mental body. When used in concert with calcite and pyrite, it helps to integrate mind and spirit. It, as well as calcite, is also good for teeth and bones.

Pyrite

Pyrite assists in the grounding or physical assimilation of the various shifts and processes of change occurring to the mental body during spiritual growth. It helps bring high vibrational unfoldments and changes into physical expression.

Lapis Lazuli

Lapis is a very potent and important brow chakra opening crystal. Its use has been known back into antiquity, with the Egyptians and other cultures utilizing it.

The crystals and stones listed below are *extremely* useful "openers and vibration raisers." They are powerful and the user may need to allow for periods of rest between uses. This is a highly individualized thing, and your "way" of using them will become obvious after purchase.

Kunzite

Kunzite is a very high vibrational heart chakra activator. It has a very high, still, and spacious vibration and is highly useful as it will rapidly assist in opening the heart chakra. As this opening is the "heart of the matter" in regards to spiritual growth, I highly recommend the use of Kunzite.

Moldavite

Here is probably one of the most important vibrational tools available today, and you can purchase it very inexpensively. Moldavite is a tektite, of meteoritic origin, and is an all around "vibration raiser" and "opener." It affects people in widely variant ways, suited perfectly, of course, for the individual.

Danburite

Danburite is a very high vibrational stone and can be utilized for opening and cleansing any area, but is especially good for the solar plexus, heart, third eye, and crown and above chakras.

Although it is not mentioned in the literature currently available, this crystal is *very* good for helping to cleanse and open the **solar plexus chakra**, a crucial element during the unfoldment process. This stone, like clear quartz, is an all-around opener, empowerer, and cleanser, and can be utilized anywhere.

Sugilite

A deep purple stone, Sugilite is a high vibrational "third eye and above" opener. Very useful and popular stone.

There are, of course, countless other crystals. For information on these, consult one of the very good crystal books that can be easily located at a metaphysical book store. A good example of one of these is **Crystal Enlightenment** by Katrina Raphaell. There are also various versions of "crystal encyclopedias" that can be quickly obtained, as usage of crystals is widely known and accepted in contemporary metaphysical circles. **Crystal Co-Creators** by Dorothy Roeder is an example of a comprehensive and well-done "crystal encyclopedia."

Western Esoteric Devices

Now we come to a fascinating area of spiritual/scientific research that is little known outside certain circles. Many individuals in the West, at different points in history, have uncovered knowledge of prana, the life-force. Of course, they have all utilized different names to describe this primary, all-pervasive consciousness-energy. Vril, Odic Force, Vital Force, Orgone energy and countless others have been utilized. Here is an important and fundamental consideration: *all of these names describe the same energy*! Here are a couple of useful esoteric devices that come from these brave studies - there are many more.

The Orgone Blanket

This has been discussed earlier in this chapter, so we won't rehash the information. I would only say that this simple device, easily constructed by anyone with materials found in their own home, can *substantially* improve and add to an individual's health and quality of life, by its passive use alone. From my experience, the only restrictor to the use of this device is ignorance. Unless one is sensitized and can perceive, to whatever degree, the flow of the life energy, one is likely to think that this device has no value and does not work. I can assure you, as can anyone who can feel the energy flow, that this is a useful device which operates *whether or not the individual can perceive energetic flows.*

Biocircuits

In the early 20th century, a man by the name of Leon Eeman invented some simple devices which helped him to overcome chronic injury sustained in WW I. These, devices, now known as **biocircuits**, directly balance the polar (Yin-Yang) aspects of the energetic bodies of humans. They are very powerful and are constructed of copper or silk, which are both conductors of the life-force or chi. These two materials conduct two different energetic spectrums or vibrational components of the life energy, the copper operating on a lower energetic spectrum and the silk on high vibrational energies.

The biocircuit, like the Orgone blanket, is a passive device. It is used in a prone position and will quickly balance a person's energetic bodies in a short period of time, bringing about a state of deep relaxation, energetic equanimity, and increased internal stillness. *I highly recommend the use of biocircuits* as they are useful in assisting meditation practice as well as promoting a rapid unfoldment of consciousness. They are very useful in reducing the stress of everyday life in the physical reality.

Biocircuits are easy to construct at home, you can make either a copper or silk one in an afternoon or evening. For an excellent book that includes construction information and lots of background see **Biocircuits** by Leslie Patten.

There are many other Western esoteric devices ... look around for them and you'll find them. Try 'em out and see if they are useful and fun, and if so, employ them in your practice.

Physical Exercise

This section wouldn't be complete without a word about a practice that seems to most to be very *non-spiritual*, physical exercise. Through the use of many of the above mentioned techniques, you will be accessing increasing volumes of prana and will need to integrate this into the physical reality. Exercise, on top of granting the practitioner a good overall level of health, greatly assists in integrating these energies into the physical body.

Essentially, as the channeled information indicated, all of these techniques and processes are opening the individual to greater and greater flows of prana. The increased prana then is employed in the **refinement of the cerebrospinal system**, which is the method by which higher states of consciousness can be accessed while in physical form. Physical exercise greatly assists in this process.

Walking is an excellent exercise because it is a "Yin-Yang" activity and so inherently energizing. It is easy to do with a minimum of equipment. A walk of a half an hour to an hour a day is an wonderful practice. Or at least three times a week, if time constraints interfere.

Bicycling is also excellent exercise and good fun, as well as possessing the added benefit of treating the rider to a more rapidly changing panorama of scenery to enjoy. Once again, a half an hour to an hour a day will keep anyone fit and hasten energetic integration. In order to reap the benefits of exercise, it is necessary that it be continuous for some useful period of time, in order to get the bodily systems, including the circulatory system, operating at a "higher than resting" level.

A couple of other good exercises to mention would include swimming and cross country skiing. The most important thing is to discover something you enjoy and will stick with and then do it.

Well, that about does it for my spiritual practice recommendations. There are, of course, many other practices that you can discover and employ. As with physical exercise, one of the fundamental considerations is that you utilize practices that you enjoy and find fun in or they will not be continued, which is the basis of progress and unfoldment. In order for the techniques to work, they must be employed on a regular basis. These techniques do work, as countless practitioners will attest, but the “proof” of their value for you will only come from your own use and experience.

Other Realities

"The planes of union are wonder."
Shiva Sutras I-12

A casual examination of any body of spiritual literature will expose the individual to information and discussion concerning various **non-physical realities**. As we are essentially non-physical Beings, our True Home is not of this earth, and we merely come here for experiences leading to growth. The various realities that comprise the manifested realms can be thought of as a spectrum of consciousness, with the physical reality being the most "dense" or lowest vibrational component in this spectrum. The higher vibrational realities have been called by many names, and one finds varying numbers and descriptions of them. I personally adhere to the school of thought advanced by various saints and metaphysicians of India, in which there are seven manifested realms, corresponding to the seven chakras or energy centers found expressed in humans. The realm immediately "higher" in vibration than ours is generally referred to as the Astral Plane and is the realm that evolving souls return to between incarnations. Each human has experienced many **cycles** of "life" (physical incarnation) and "death" (presence in the Astral or other realms), a process that can be seen to be analogous to Day and Night, or any other cycle observed in nature.

These realms can be conceptualized as consisting of increasing refinement of consciousness and rate of vibration as one ascends through the hierarchy. In my channeling activities, I obtained information concerning some but not all of these realms. For clarity, here are the names utilized in order of increasing vibration: Physical Plane, Astral (or Emotional) Plane, Mental Plane, Causal or Intuitive Realities. The last term encompasses more than one plane or realm, and indicates a high level of consciousness refinement.

As interesting and wonderful as knowledge concerning these "Higher Realms" or other realities might be, it is important to emphasize that **Paradise pervades Everything and it is Here Now!**

Thus it is important to live in the present, as many spiritual traditions advocate.

Describe and discuss the Astral Plane.

If we view the spectrum of consciousness like a spectrum of visible light (or a rainbow) the various "planes" or Realities of Existence can be thought of as bands of consciousness in a Rainbow of Consciousness. As with a physical spectrum, the different levels or bands represent differing frequencies of consciousness. While incarnate in the Physical Plane of existence, the individualized unit of consciousness, in most cases, focuses on the PHYSICAL EXTERNALS, believing the reality and the objects in it to be the only reality.

Because the physical world is a realm of dense vibration, an individual must begin spiritual practice of one modality or another in order to refine the "detector of consciousness," the cerebrospinal system, to a level at which it can begin to RESONATE WITH DIFFERENT FREQUENCIES OF CONSCIOUSNESS. While it is true that many people who are incarnate in physical form have done this and are able to operate at higher levels of consciousness, it is not true that any large number of humans have reached this condition as of this point in linear time.

When the "astral" vehicle or body of consciousness is activated, the individual is able to "travel astrally" ... leaving his physical body in his astral body for the purpose of "touring" or exploration of the Astral realm, the band of consciousness immediately higher in vibration than the Physical Plane. The Astral Plane is characterized by many features that would seem impossible and/or alien in the physical realm ... including "more flexible" or more subjective experience of time (this is because the Astral is "closer in vibration" to the higher realms where, ultimately, there is no linear time, nothing but the NOW). Additionally, individuals have much more ability to travel through use of INTENTION ... that is, desire to be at some imagined place and appear there effortlessly.

The Astral realm is also described as the Emotional Realm and this is because the frequency of consciousness represented by this realm concerns the emotions and emotional body of man. Now this does not mean that everyone is suddenly completely emotional all the time, no more than being incarnate in the physical means that one is merely physical all the time. The experience of the individualized unit of consciousness in *any* realm will be determined by THE DEVELOPMENT OF THE VARIOUS "BODIES" OR VEHICLES OF CONSCIOUSNESS of that particular individual.

It is true that those who of a "low" vibration will find themselves RESONATING with a similar "low" frequency vibration in the Astral world ... i.e. close to the Physical Plane and in regions not at all to be desired (these are the Hells of various religions). However, as you know, time in any manifested realm is of a TEMPORARY nature, so after some time spent in the "lower regions" the individualized unit of consciousness will find himself slowly, through time and experience, vibrating in resonance with higher and higher levels of consciousness. Thus he will eventually find himself in the wonderful (when compared to the physical) upper regions of the Astral Plane and would experience a glowing, flowing spectrum of gauzy light that really is quite the thing to behold.

While it is true that these realms are very pleasant and beautiful, they are by no means the most beautiful of the manifested realms, as you might suspect. That privilege is reserved for what you might call the Intuitive Realities (sometimes called the Devachan). In these realities highly evolved teacher/beings that have sometimes been called Angels or Devas dwell. They are engaged in the work of "spreading the news" concerning the nature of the higher realities and God (or Supreme Consciousness). The Astral reality is, like all the manifested realities, a wonderland to play in once one has developed the ability to do so.

Discuss and describe the Mental Realm or Plane.

Well, the Mental Piane, unlike the Astral Plane is dominated by an experience of INSTANTANEOUS MANIFESTATION OF THOUGHT-FORMS. What I mean by this is that whatever one is engaged in thinking about is instantly created. Now, for you in physical incarnation, this can sound like a dangerous dynamic, and it would be if available to the inhabitants of the Physical Plane. However, *a certain level of "evolution" (or unfoldment) of consciousness is required* before one will find resonance with this level of Being. This means that those that would misuse this ability will not find themselves present in this realm.

Once again, the experience of dwelling within the Mental Realm is very difficult to communicate to one incarnated in the Physical Plane because there are generally no points of reference with which the unit of consciousness will be familiar unless they engage in spiritual practice. The essence of some of the experiential life in these higher realms is really beyond description in words, except to say that flow, light, connection, Love and Joy characterize this as well as the highest manifested realms. It is merely a matter of degree, you see.

While it could be said that those inhabitants of the Physical Plane that develop their cerebrospinal system sufficiently can have firsthand experiential knowledge of these realms, one might consider that their essence can be best understood by the RESONATING INHABITANTS of any particular realm. You will find that those that understand the Physical Realm of existence best are generally those that perform the best within it and understand that one must ACCORD with certain requirements in order to "live well." These include: assuring for economic survival, adequate maintenance of the physical form through eating well, physical exercise and taking care of oneself in general by minimizing stress, worry, anger and all of the "negative" or destructive (separative) energies.

This is also true of those that accord best with the higher realms ... they understand the basic nature of the realm and what must be done to flow or resonate in harmony with the particular realm. A general description of this realm is that it is more substantially full of the Innate Qualities and hence, those that are having the experience of Being in it enjoy greater access to these qualities which would include Bliss, Love, Peace, Truth, Joy, etc.

The inhabitant of the Mental Realm perceives it to be full of interconnecting "light" or consciousness and enjoys the ESSENTIAL HARMONY OF CONSCIOUS INTERCONNECTION. This is, once again, more true of the even higher realms. So you see the nature of the spectrum of consciousness ... as one moves "higher," one experiences MORE of what already pervades Everything but they merely EXPERIENCE IT CONSCIOUSLY instead of at a deeper level of existence, which is what the bulk of humanity does now.

More on the Mental Realm?

If we consider that humanity is poised on the brink of an adventure so great as to be unprecedented in the entire history of mankind and the planet, we can comprehend that the essence of the higher realms is one of INCREASED ATTRIBUTES OF PURE CONSCIOUSNESS. As a sparrow must fly in the air to achieve FREEDOM, so must the human unit of consciousness explore the uncharted (generally) realms of Spirit.

The Mental Realm is one of DIRECT MANIFESTATION OF THOUGHT. Other than this generalization, not much more can be offered that will be comprehended as, once again, we're starting to get into an area of non-conceptual reality wherein the concepts sometimes merely get in the way. If I were to say that the Mental Realm is characterized by "flowing Essence" and great interconnection, this would make some sense, but would not describe the experience of "being" in the Mental Realm. Therefore, an attempt is made to generalize as much as is possible in terms that will be understood.

Most experiences in higher realms are more UNLIMITED than can be described through the use of words and concepts. Think of pure light ... its expansive, brilliant, glowing nature .... its ability to be in many places at one time. Physical light is an ANALOG for the type of light/consciousness that exists in the higher realms pervasively and instantaneously. While it is true that it is impossible to completely grasp the essence of these realms without DIRECT EXPERIENCE, it is also true that these generalized descriptions utilizing words can be helpful because they provide a glimpse (conceptually) of the reality being discussed.

Discuss the Causal or Intuitive Realities.

Well, once again, Mark, we're getting into weirder and weirder territory from the perspective of the Physical Plane of existence. The Causal realm is characterized by INTUITIVE

TRANSFER OF INFORMATION through the use of symbols and "light-talk" (consciousness transference). More than this it is hard to comment on except to say that these are the realms of the Devas and, as such, spectacular in a beauty that is beyond earthly comprehension.

One might say that flowing "Beings of Light" dance in a wonder-ballet of Love. Visualize the most shining, glowing, radiant Beings that you can and place them in a swirling miasma of love consciousness and you will, once again, have a CONCEPTUAL CONSTRUCT that may assist somewhat, but does not do justice to the realm in question. Now, one may think that this means that one should not try to conceptualize these things ... but this is not the case, one must merely understand the LIMITATION of mental conceptualization.

When one is a resident of the Devachan, one is an interconnected Being of Light and is in great harmony with All That Exists and the specific band of consciousness that constitutes the realm. If we can visualize this type of existence, then we can help to try to actualize it more in the lower realms, as this would be of great benefit.

Describe the Devas or Angels.

If we think of the Play of Consciousness as PLAY, then we can see that the Devic beings or Angels are engaged in a very high form of play. As has been stated before, the Devachan is very difficult to describe from the perspective of the Physical Plane of existence. One could discuss flowing sheets of Light, much like your Aurora Borealis, but this would merely be an analogy and only give a hint of the spectacular beauty present in this realm of existence.

The "life" of a Deva is simple, it is engaged in celebration, or expression of Joy and Love, through the medium of sharing or teaching with beings of many different sorts. One could not say that the Devas are doing this for any other reason than it provides and/or expresses the Pure Joy of Being. Once again, this is one of the incredible and great secrets ... do what it is that gives you Joy and you will AUTOMATICALLY ASSIST every other being, as this is simply the "nature of reality" or "how things work."

In the swimming Sea of Consciousness, there are many condensed expressions of Pure Consciousness, and these are going about activities the purpose of which, to put in terms understandable in your realm, is merely THE CELEBRATION OF THE PURE "BEINGNESS" OF ALL THINGS. These activities may directly provide service to other beings, or they may merely provide distant, indirect service of a nature that, from the perspective of your realm, it is very difficult to define the activities as "service" at all. No matter. As long as the beings will merely seek out and do those things that give them Joy, they will be working for the greater good.

This simple concept is DIRECTLY AGAINST PREVAILING THOUGHT-FORMS in your mass consciousness and so it is very difficult to convince the individualized essence of consciousness that this is "the Way." However, all they must do is merely try it for themselves and see if their lives turn 'round a new corner and head off in different directions. The essence of fully enjoying life is simple: RELAX INTO ANY CIRCUMSTANCE YOU ENCOUNTER AND ENJOY IT FULLY, even "bad" dynamics or circumstances.

As the manifested realms are merely the Expressed Dance of Consciousness set into play for the experience of the individualized units of consciousness, including humans, then nothing can harm the ESSENTIAL, ENDURING NATURE of any being. Once this is finally grasped at a deep level, the individual "relaxes into" life in general and experiences a more peaceful perspective with which to view reality.

Speak to this: "Human beings are Beings of Light."

If we consider that the Essential Nature of The Great Wholeness is energy, consciousness, or Light, we can say we some degree of certainty that EVERYTHING IS (WONDERFULLY) LIGHT!! There is no lack of Light anywhere ... what there is a lack of is the knowledge of Light, or spiritual knowledge. You would think that people would not find it difficult to embrace themselves as Light, but this is nonetheless the case, because when people come here, they OVER-IDENTIFY WITH THE BODY AND THE MIND (as you know).

This is no big deal, it merely means that they then are often constrained to suffer, because they view this realm of existence as THE ONLY ONE and feel that everything must be played out in this realm of physicality. However, as you know, this is not the case. This is merely a realm of experience which constitutes a PLAYGROUND OF THE INFINITE FOR CONSCIOUSNESS UNITS!!

Discuss the term "light body" as it is currently used in the metaphysical literature.

The term "light body" is simply used to describe the higher aspects of the energetic system of man. You will find that the light body describes the "pure white light" aspects or those aspects that express the highest levels of consciousness or God etc. It could be said that the current craze for this term in the literature is generated by the increasingly intense infusion of energy into the realm of the Physical Plane at this point in time.

As you know, this is a time of "rising energy" and this is the very dynamic that enables so many people, such as yourself, to make such great progress in the realm of spirituality. The light body is a very good descriptive phrase to illuminate one of the basic and yet, to date, highly unknown aspects of the human race. This phrase enables us to visualize the Essential Nature of mankind as light or energy. This energy body contains within it differing states of vibration which are reflective of the individual's level of evolution of consciousness.

What is termed the "light body" is an aspect of the highest order and can be equated with purity, God, Supreme Consciousness, Bliss, and other descriptions which pertain to the great Reality which pervades all. You might say that the light body is a good contemporary term, as it captures the imagination and, once again, is a visual term. In the end we are all "adding light," or higher aspects of consciousness, to our individualized consciousness essence. I would say that the light body concept is a good one that helps to remove fear and encourage exploration of the simple aspects of the spiritual world.

Discuss in descriptive terms the concept "Realms of Light."

Well, what one could say regarding Realms of Light is that they exist all around everyone at all times. While it is true that there are many spectacular sights in the higher realms, it could be said that EVERYONE IS NOW LIVING IN PARADISE, wherever they are, and it is merely illusion that prevents them from fully realizing this.

The conceptualization of Realms of Light or "heaven" in your world is dominated by cultural and religious projection. It could be said that in Realms of Light everything is a shimmering spectacle of consciousness, that things FLOW in a most wonderful and beautiful way, and that individualized units of consciousness are going about the duty and process of celebration.

There is nothing to the manifested realms except Joy, Bliss, Love, Truth, etc. and the perception of this reality has been mucked with by the emotional and mental fields of those incarnate in your world who, due to OVER-INVOLVEMENT WITH MATTER, mistakenly assume everything to be SEPARATE and not as it is - an essential connected UNITY. If we can see that the totality of existence is comprised of the totality of existence, we can then see that the individualized parts of existence are engaged in a segmented play of the Whole.

The higher realms, being places of greater "Being" or consciousness or higher vibration, are much more subtle and refined than your realm of dense vibration. Those that dwell in these realms know the inexpressible quality of beauty that pervades them and the inhabitants utilize NON-PHYSICAL SENSING APPARATUS to appreciate this beauty and, as such, it is very hard to describe the beauty of these realms to those incarnate in the Physical Plane of existence.

Speak to human beings as Immortal Spirits.

The human unit of consciousness is an IMMORTAL SPIRITUAL CONDENSATION OF PURE CONSCIOUSNESS. Endeavoring to live from this place will, simply and easily, put one in a place of FLOW of consciousness in which one automatically does not "take things too seriously" and demonstrates detachment or non-attachment to the circumstances and conditions of the Physical Plane, which merely amount to the expressed Play of Consciousness.

We are in the middle of an incredible transformatory time, and many people will have experiences that will lead them to a place of KNOWLEDGE through Realization of their Innate or True Nature. This is a very groovy thang, which everyone gets a real boot out of and there is no place of fear attached, as FEAR IS OF THE LOWER MIND and these innate states of Being far transcend such a consciousness restrictor as fear.

In the middle of the process that is known as remembrance or Self-Realization, the individualized condensation of Pure Consciousness will often go through some periods of "dense vibration," or difficulty, as lower vibrational or "negative" energies are removed naturally or cleansed from the system. One is always best off if one merely "rides the tiger" and *relaxes into any of these circumstances,* as they cannot harm you in the least. Merely OBSERVE as these things occur and ENJOY as much as possible.

Is the reason that the future is so hard to predict because it is a field of probabilities when viewed from this realm and so as things change in this realm the possible future changes?

Well OK! The essence of the future, as viewed from your realm, is that it is in continuous flux. It can be considered a FIELD OF PROBABILITY, and as such, it is highly subject to the actions and conditions occurring within the very realm being considered for future prediction. Those individuals who become very adept at prognostication are very few indeed ... a certain level of spiritual attainment and the ability to consider many differing energy factors must be developed.

It could be said that in your realm, the future is best considered as a RANGE OF PROBABLE FUTURES, all of which are possibilities and subject to the actions taken by the people involved. You will find that too much concern or speculation about the future is counterproductive, for, as you know, it is best to be fully alive in the NOW.

Comment on the "dense vibrational" nature of the Physical Plane.

What one could say is that this describes a NECESSARY circumstance in the Physical Plane because *the Physical Plane, like all manifested realms, is merely a construct designed for the purposes of growth.* There is no other use or reason for the existence of the Physical Plane. Hence it follows that, if you're going to design a realm whose major intention is rapid growth, then it might be good to make it a "difficult" place where one must learn to triumph over all sorts of PERCEIVED lacks and other "dense vibration" issues.

The unit of consciousness will then, after many incarnated lives, reach a point of evolution wherein it will grasp that the essence of everything manifest is COMPLETENESS OR WHOLENESS and, in doing this "grasping" will reach a point of understanding in which he will demonstrate the required level of growth to "leave" or "not return to" the Physical Plane ... in other words, he's graduated!

It can be understood that the nature of Consciousness is such that everything is comprised merely of consciousness in different dresses and disguises so that the "dense vibrational" consciousness of the Physical Plane is *always under the complete control of the individualized expressions of pure consciousness that live there.* As has been earlier discussed, this is the essence of "mind science." The mind is merely a "higher vibrational" expression of Consciousness and, as such, is able to manipulate or manifest activity in the denser vibrational dynamic of the manifested Physical Plane.

The Great Wholeness - Everything is One Thing

"The various systems of philosophy merely expound
and interpret the different aspects of this Reality
from different points of view."
Pratyabhijna Hridayam - Sutra VIII

For many thousands of years various sages of different cultures have understood that a Great Unity supports and underlies everything that is. They understood that you can call this Great Wholeness by any name or no name, as you like. Every single extant religion is referring to this **same underlying Reality**, the fact of which reduces all of the "Holy" wars fought throughout history to pure goofy absurdity. Ancient Wisdom is coming to light during these very interesting times and this assists in realizing the nature of this Reality through teachings and esoteric practices which lead to an experiential understanding. Today one can go into any bookstore and find "how-to" texts on Kundalini and Taoist Yoga, once both only the provenance of initiates and monks through oral transmission.

Consciousness is the stuff and fabric of all manifested creation. Everything around you in the room as you read this book is consciousness in different forms and frequencies of vibration. We are living in a Sea of Pure Consciousness and through refinement of the cerebrospinal system we can consciously swim in this Ocean and join in the party.

The Infinite is, by definition, beyond Limits. Words and concepts are limited and so may only serve to give a glimpse into the fundamental Reality, call it God, Tao, Pure Consciousness, All That Is or whatever. However, I have received much channeled information on the Great Wholeness and consciousness and feel that it is interesting and useful to pass this along, and so I do.

Speak on Pure Consciousness.

While it could be said that there is nothing BUT Pure Consciousness, the individualized unit of consciousness will experience various degrees of realization concerning this fact. When we examine Pure Consciousness from the perspective of the higher realms, we find that it is ubiquitously discussed and understood on an intuitive level. This is probably the area of the most misunderstanding during an individual's awakening: *these things must be understood on a "right brain," "subjective" or intuitive level.*

The essence of Pure Consciousness is that it IS ... it exists, it is BEING. The ability to accord with Existence Nature is what you would sometimes term as Spiritual Growth .... acceptance of the All *as it is*, Love of the physical world and everything in it, knowledge of the Essential Nature of All Things as energy or consciousness, an intuitive grasp of the essentially UNSEPARATED nature of everything. You will find that each culture, as you already know, generates or "comes up with" various perspectives, viewpoints or approaches from which to understand the essence of the spiritual world and Pure Consciousness. These methods (called religions by you) are useful AS LONG AS THEY DO NOT INTRODUCE OR PERPETUATE FEAR, as this is the great "cloud across the sun," so to speak.

It is not understood in our culture that one should "shop around" through the various religions and systems of philosophy and pick one (or several) that suit them ... comment?

Well, what we could say is that, of course, in your realm people have been CONDITIONED mentally to view the approach of their parents and/or the culture as "the one true way," etc. and this, understandably, causes no small amount of fear in the individual when they attempt to break away from this essentially fear-based perspective. What is required is a level of "adventure mentality" or exploration or realization that one does not have to be constrained to any one perspective and can choose that perspective or perspectives THAT SERVE THEM PERSONALLY. As Roy Eugene Davis has said, human beings are superior to what they perceive.

With this in mind, it can be easily seen that the individualized unit of consciousness should "go toward" those things that it feels attracted to or has an affinity with because these things will enable *the greatest growth with the least fear.*

Discuss the concept of "The Whole" and Wholeness.

My, my ... we are coming up with some lulus today, aren't we? If we consider that All That Is comprises a Great Wholeness of Everything (somewhat redundant, eh?), then we can see that this Wholeness is the Natural Order of things ... nothing more, nothing less. When we can see, on an individual basis, that in order to live a fuller, more "whole" life all we must do is to *relax into the Whole*, then things start to change in wonderful ways for the individual.

As it is the case that there is nothing outside this Wholeness, then ALL THINGS ARE GOOD AND PERFECT, there are no defective things AT ALL, anywhere. What is perceived as "defective" or "lacking" is perceived so because of INCOMPLETE INFORMATION, usually concerning the dynamics of energy/consciousness and how everything works at a basic or Intrinsic level.

Now, there are those who would come to the conclusion that things are not perfect based on the level of pain and suffering that exists in the Physical Plane, but, once again, this position comes from lack of information. What can harm a Being of Pure Consciousness? Nothing! The things that occur, as we have discussed, in the Physical Plane are merely EXPERIENCES FOR CONSCIOUSNESS UNITS and do not harm the Essential Nature of anyone, merely their physical expression.

On the journey back to Wholeness, or Spiritual Remembrance, many people will come to the conclusion that everything is PERFECT as it is and start to relax into wherever they find themselves more. This does not mean that one should not try to help one's fellow pilgrims. It merely means that one can help them more by explaining the nature of Reality, so that aspect of themselves which is ALREADY AWARE OF THIS can begin to resonate with it, and they may start to journey back to knowledge of the Whole Oneness that is Life.

What practical tips do you have for maximizing the knowledge that "Everything is Perfect" in terms of daily life?

As it is the case that the individualized condensation of Pure Consciousness is on a unique and distinct path that THEY WILL GROOVE WITH AND LOVE, once they figure out that there is now, and never has been, anything to be afraid of or concerned with, we can see that the perception that "Everything is Perfect" will slowly and PERFECTLY dawn upon them. In the meantime, one can actualize behavior that will support this Reality by doing the following things:

1. RELAX NOW ... NOT LATER! This is the most important dynamic that will increase enjoyment of anyone at any time and it should be actualized whenever possible, as there is nothing to be concerned about for an IMMORTAL ENERGY BEING!

2. EXPLORE those aspects and avenues of yourself that are not currently known to you for when you do you will see that there is nothing to be concerned with here, either. The individual is a PERFECT condensation of PERFECTION, so they are Perfect now, they are Perfect later ... they are ALWAYS PERFECT. One might ask: "Why is it the case that I don't see or feel this already extant Perfection?" And the answer is that they are trying to "bring about" or "expecting" certain results that may or may not be the "highest" or "most groovy" thing at the present time.

EVERYTHING IS OCCURRING PERFECTLY, so what is occurring is the right and Perfect thing at that moment in time and the "secret" is to merely *accord with or quietly observe this Perfection* without overly desiring some preconceived result or outcome. This is what is known as "Going with the Flow" ... i.e. one merely "flows with" whatever is happening at a particular moment in time. This can also be viewed as RELAXING INTO THE PRESENT.

3. Utilization of the various techniques that are available to BRING THE ATTENTION INTO THE PRESENT AND ONTO WHATEVER IS OCCURRING. When one does this, it Stills the

mind and brings about a place of "calm focused concentration," as you know from playing music. In this place there is nothing but concentration, i.e. there is no "time" for the individual to generate mental concerns about anything at all. SUFFERING IS OF THE MIND, as the Buddha said and as you know. It is always a good practice to let go of bothersome mental things, once you have observed them, because then the consciousness merely returns to WHAT IT ALWAYS IS, without the modification of the lower mental body.

4. If we consider that one can actualize the highest life for oneself at the moment by merely ACCEPTING THE ALL AS IT IS, UNCONDITIONALLY, we can see that this is a fine and wonderful goal to aim for and attempt to actualize. *That is - Love everything now!!* There is nothing "wrong" or "lacking" or "occurring too slowly" or "harmful." There are only experiences in the lower realms, so one can do himself a favor and MERELY EN-JOY THE EXPERIENCES, whatever they are. Do this whenever possible and the knowledge that everything is perfect will spontaneously come forth.

The lower mind, being an instrument of individualized separation and experience gathering, will *attempt to defend or protect itself* from perceived lack and fears causing a CONDITION OF CONTRACTION OF CONSCIOUSNESS. This is diametrically opposed to the state of "relaxed Being in Love" that is characteristic of the highly evolved. When one notices a fear, one can *immediately let go of it*, as it is "not of them" as Innate Essence, and merely RESTRICTS instead of EXPANDS.

OK .... how about some tips on taking action and seeing results in a sea of Pure Consciousness?

Good question ... what I would say is that there is nothing to do except these things:

1. TAKE WHATEVER ACTION YOU FEEL DRAWN TO NOW. Don't wait around, especially with something you feel drawn to. Merely make or take the action in an effortless, FLOWING

manner because this is the way of according with Flowing Fields of Light, which as you know, is all that exists.

2. SIT BACK AND ENJOY YOURSELF!! Don't fret, don't strive ... merely take whatever action you will and then observe. As it is the case that nothing is separate in this Flowing Field of Light, then we can see that things will simply manifest in a COMPLETE or WHOLE manner, nothing less. This is why it is advised in spiritual practice to not be attached to results. What is imperfect in a big field of interconnected Light?

What this means is that it is "more Innate" to merely take the action you desire ... any action, don't limit yourself, and then ACCORD WITH or ENJOY whatever results take place. If you remain attached to some result or another, you will find that this is the way of limitation and suffering. *The universe, being comprised only of conscious Love/Light is completely supportive and beneficent* ... in other words, things are always heading toward the highest place of pure grooviness for every individual and the collective Great Wholeness. Just do what you will and then GROOVE WITH THE FLOW or outcome/result.

Discuss and describe the nature of the soul.

The human soul is a CONDENSATION OF PURE CONSCIOUSNESS. It contains within its energy/consciousness structure the blueprint or life make-up of the specific attributes of the individualization of consciousness that the person is. In other words, what the person *essentially is*, in terms of their UNIQUE EXPRESSION (also can be viewed as an Aspect of the One), is found at the level of the soul or causal body.

If we consider that each Being is essentially *both* an aspect of Consciousness *and* attribute-less (or transcendent) consciousness itself, we can see that like many other things in life a BALANCE is required between these two Being-states. Many advanced yogis have attained the place of merged freedom, or complete transcendence in which, and let's be clear here, there is no desire to leave the Ocean of Pure Bliss as an individualized Being. However, YOU ARE "THAT" NOW .... this cannot be stressed enough.

Now, there exist certain tactics and techniques, used by various spiritual teachers historically, which are aimed at crushing or destroying the SENSE OF SEPARATE EXISTENCE, not the "Beingness" of the individual, which cannot be done, as every Being is a Ray of the Infinite Consciousness and is, hence, omnipresent and Immortal NOW!! As you have discerned, the problem with these techniques is they initially generate a place of more fear or constriction which can lead to a resolution beyond the mind. However, it can generate a place of temporarily increased suffering and is not at all necessary to bring the Being home.

EMBRACEMENT IS THE WAY OF SHIVA. What this means is that the person merely "loves everything" or "includes everything" as a part of their Being, which *is the truth of their being now*, and in doing this, experiences an EXPANSION wherein they see themselves in others and become more connected. The "bashing" method causes initial constriction resolving into expansion, but since what we are trying to do is to expand past the limits of identification with the body, mind, thoughts, forms, ideas, etc., this constrictive game is not really with the program at this point of time in history and simply should BE SEEN FOR WHAT IT IS ... A TECHNIQUE! There is no need to spend any time "sitting with it" for those who are not drawn toward it. Some people come to feel a need to have their sense of separation broken in this way.

To continue on the soul. The soul *is* the essence of the person NOW, or it is what they really are. It is omniscient and omnipresent because, although it could be conceptualized as a star or container of Light, it is condensed from the Light all around it, which it is in constant contact with, of course. This is an important point - *there is no difference between the Soul and the Oversoul in terms of their makeup* - they are Consciousness and are One.

There is an old analogy - it is like a balloon full of water that is in the Ocean. The water, which is what you are *now*, does not care whether it is in the balloon or whether it is in the Ocean because the Ocean is NOT DIFFERENT from it - *it is all just water*, or Consciousness, if you get my drift. The thing that is scared by certain concepts, techniques, etc. - IS THE CONTAINER, which is also consciousness, but in a contracted form. In this constricted form it is LIMITED, and does not have the ability to grasp that which it is and is "broadcasting" it or generating it. Instead, it thinks that everything is about those things that it perceives, which can be understood to be sense inputs and ideas occurring within itself. It is like a self-contained processing machine for operation as a separated being.

The problems begin when the being which is USING the mind and body, YOU, starts to OVER-IDENTIFY with them and *forgets* that it is Pure Conscious Light without any essential FORM. It is the hang-up with form that is causing such a big deal problem in the world today, as if a form would ever need "protection" for an Immortal condensation of consciousness. In the end, all words are futile to completely demonstrate and explain this, and one can make their journey much easier by TRUSTING that they will like the place they are headed to greatly, because it is an already extant state where they already are, at a higher level of being.

In the Grand Dance of Consciousness, there are many souls. These souls are DIFFERENT ASPECTS OF THE ABSOLUTE and there is essentially no difference, in terms of conceptualization, if you conceptualize them as points of light like a star or merely "coming forth" out of the Infinite Body of the Absolute like a cloud comes forth from an empty sky. The soul is the EXPRESSIVE ASPECT of the Absolute, and as such, IS the Absolute. This concept causes no small means of goofiness in your realm, where people have been conditioned that they and God are separate and that to BE GOD is pure blasphemy. This is complicated further by any "ego bashing" technique that makes the person "feel bad" about their personality self as this is a place of contraction instead of their already extant nature of TOTAL EXPANSION.

This is a very confused area in the minds of Western people, for when a spiritual teacher tells you "you are nothing, go away" he means that you are "NO - THING," Pure Consciousness, Light; and not a body, mind or any form. However, in the West, people have been told by parents and society that they are "nothing," which means "you have no worth" in terms of the human culture of "doingness." Everyone has INTRINSIC WORTH, beyond any culture or anything they would do, because they are a PART OF THE INFINITE or God, whichever term you choose. Do something or do nothing, you now have and will always have worth of an unlimited nature, which is completely unknown to the struggling mass of society.

When the person realizes their soul-nature, they are said to have attained the place of Self-realization (although there, as usual, is some confusion of terms with this term being applied to various states of more transcendent consciousness). This is a very groovy place and the person that has attained the constant state of soul awareness will not feel any threat or concern from any event or circumstance occurring in any realm of existence, as they realize that they are SUPERIOR to things that they perceive, as Roy E. Davis says. They realize, fully, their Immortality and the Immortality of all Beings. They remain in a place of Joy, Love, contentment and happiness that is Self-complete and not dependent on external occurrences of any kind - it is a state of complete happiness.

There are states of consciousness above this level, but by the time a Being reaches this level he no longer suspects that there will be any "catch" in this whole WONDERFUL world of Consciousness.

Discuss and describe, then, the Ultimate State of Reality.

Very good question, Mr. Spaciousness! For that is the Ultimate State - an Infinite Sea of Existence/Being which is completely *free of any attributes.* This is the state referred to in the metaphysics of India as the Absolute or the Transcendent (Unmanifest) Field of Pure Consciousness. This is also known as the Void and is called "Inherent Emptiness" by the Buddhists. It contains NO THING, and yet is the Fullest possible state of Pure Potentiality.

This place of Being is completely beyond the grasp of the mind and can only be directly experienced, not conceptualized - so don't try! Merely RELAX as much as possible and, at the exactly right moment, the Realization of this deeply Innate place will dawn.

From this condition springs the First Source which is called "God" in the West and by various names in the East including Brahma, Pure Consciousness, Clear Light of Bliss, Tao, etc. This First Source is the *actively manifesting* aspect of the Absolute. The Sea of God is an Infinite (omnipresent), omniscient, and omnipotent field of Consciousness and contains specific *Innate attributes* including Love, Peace, Joy, Bliss, etc. It is the ultimate condition of MANIFESTED Reality. The Absolute manifests, but remains beyond and unaffected by its manifestations.

From the Infinite Creative Source (God), the rest of manifestation is projected by utilizing *vibration* - this is the Great Om. Everything else in manifestation in generated by this Fundamental Vibration, so obviously, *everything is simply vibrating God-Force*. Within this projecting vibrational field of Om, there are the three attributes, or gunas, discussed earlier. To refresh, these attributes are: "lightness" (sattva), "movement or dynamism" (rajas), and "heaviness" (tamas). These three attributes can be found present in everything manifested.

If we consider that, from this point in manifestation, the scientific dynamics become MUCH MORE COMPLEX and have been discussed by others in other works, we can see that it is really not necessary to dwell on the lower aspects of manifestation, but instead to have a firm grasp that All Things are One Thing, in different dresses and disguises or expressions. The dense vibrational dynamic of the Physical Plane is what is basically interfering with the individual's perception that this is the case and this is one of the "fun challenges" of coming here - to *bring Spirit or Consciousness down into this realm of density (or Darkness).*

Discuss the concept "everything is simple."

What one might say regarding this concept is that, of course everything is simple because every "thing" is merely one thing: Consciousness. The aspects, unfoldments and situational dynamics centered around the understanding of this concept are wonderful, however it is true that this is a VERY difficult concept for most people to grasp at this particular point in time.

We might view the circumstance as similar to one that is found in the belly of a whale. There is much sloshing around of various foodstuffs but in the end everything will be reduced to One Thing. While it is true that simplicity is routinely "fought" in your culture, many people are becoming more attuned to it and looking for ways to make their lives and experiences more simple.

If we view the life of the Physical Plane of existence as one in which experience is the watchword, then we can see that after some great time of various experiences, the individualized unit of consciousness begins to realize that the answers to their problems and their questions regarding the essence of "life" DO NOT LIE IN THE HAPPENINGS OF THE PHYSICAL PLANE. This is the dawning of "the awakening" in the individual, and from this point onward they become more interested in spiritual matters. What we might say is that simplicity pervades all, and that in this all-pervasive "Beingness" there is nothing but simplicity. *Complexity is merely the expression of simplicity.*

Further thoughts on "Everything is One Thing"?

"EVERYTHING IS ONE THING," as Sai Baba says, and because of this simple dynamic there is no real separation between you and the coffee table. The table is merely condensed Bliss, much in the same way that you are merely condensed Bliss .... the difference lying in the RATE OF VIBRATION AND THE QUALITY OF CONSCIOUSNESS. Everything that *is* One Thing has a highly specialized and individualized part to play in the Dance of Consciousness and this is what is known as the individual's "life purpose."

Speak to Oneness, then.

There is only One Thing and everything is an integral, non-separate part of that One Thing ... THERE IS NO "OTHER" - EVERY THING IS ONE THING. The mistaken impression which is promulgated by many spiritual paths is that there is an external "controller" (external God), but this is *incorrect* ... there is One Being, One Life, One Substance, as Roy E. Davis would say and that One Thing is Everything.

This does not imply limitation for the "parts" or "aspects" of this one thing. Instead, each individualized thing is also Unlimited, with certain specific attributes that make up its essence and are what it LOVES and IS NOW, not later. You will find that the lower mind has great difficulty completely conceptualizing this because it

SIMPLY CANNOT. It can do a fairly good job at conceptualizing Oneness by use of such terms as "no other," "everything is made of the same stuff - conscious Light," this type of thing, but it is unable to grasp the proper relationships and operating dynamics because these lie *outside its range of understanding* and are left up to the higher intuitive component to grasp. Everything is merely swimming in a Sea of Itself.

The essence of this "Everything" is merely that Every Thing consists of A SINGLE FIELD OF PURE CONSCIOUS LIGHT, so any way one wants to "name" this or describe it until they have more complete experiences of it is fine, with the "qualifier" that any term which cannot be understood as non-separate, which in your culture is often the case with the term "God," can be IGNORED.

"Light" is a good term as it is impersonal and does not imply control, which is something that we definitely want to get away from at this time because CONTROL IS NOT FREEDOM; it does not take a political science major to figure that one out!! The Field of Pure Consciousness, of which everything is an integral (read "non-separate") part is not "interested" in any sort of "agenda." It is merely *Conscious Existence, the purpose of which can be best conceptualized as Expression of Joy.*

There is no "desire" to control, there is a "desire" to EXPERIENCE and EXPRESS. These things can be best accomplished from the inherent place of freedom shared by all condensed expressions of Pure Consciousness ... to put this in the most clear way utilizing words: WHY WOULD ANYTHING WANT TO "CONTROL" OR RESTRICT ITSELF?

Speak more on this: "The Universe is completely beneficent and supportive."

And there you have it! It could best be said that the Universe is a CONSCIOUSNESS CONSTRUCT, or variously could be considered a Cosmic Dream the purpose of which is to provide realms of experience for condensed expressions of Pure Consciousness to have all sorts of surprise! ... experiences. There is no other purpose for the manifested realms. With this in mind, we can see that the processes that are occurring in the manifested realms are happening perfectly, or in RIGHT ENERGETIC RELATIONSHIP, with no lack or goofiness anywhere.

Everything is One Thing, so when the Universe, a part of that One Thing, senses that you, another part of that One Thing, need something (like money), it merely provides the required thing in *whatever form or way is the one most currently accessible.* This means that the universe is completely supportive to those who will merely relax enough to understand that there is no threat or lack!! This is the key ... there has never been any "threat" or lack and the perception that there is comes from *over-involvement* with the externals of the Physical Plane coupled with the ol' mind-emotion game.

It is the case that those individuals currently residing in the Physical Plane demonstrate all different levels of Realization of the higher truth that they are now, and always have been, Immortal spiritual beings that have come to this realm of experience to *have experiences* leading to Soul Growth. It is true that those that have begun to realize this, even if the realization is "partial" or not yet complete, will automatically DETACH somewhat from the activities and occurrences of the Physical Plane. They will understand that these experiences are not harming them and, whether or not they understand a certain experience, they are always free to IGNORE it or LET IT GO .... there's more where it came from!

Speak to "the manifested realms as holograms."

Well, certainly, and what a groovy concept this is! This is perhaps one of the best intellectual concepts that has been arrived at concerning the nature of manifested reality. The thing is, we can see that reality is a constant interplay of various diverse factors (energies or consciousness) so that when we approach "what the heck is going on" from the model of a hologram, it is apparent that the essence of what is happening involves a "reference beam" or "ground" and a "beam of reflection" or "individualized unit of consciousness." Both are necessary in the play of manifestation.

While it is true that this seems a simple mode of operation, as was just discussed, simplicity is the only game in town. As the ancients knew, "as above, so below" so that, like a hologram, each bit of manifestation contains within it the Whole. This is the Great Secret that enables the individual person to come to "know" the nature of the manifested cosmos and the transcendent levels of consciousness. These things are already known by the individual at a certain level of consciousness, and it is only the "personality" element that views these concepts as "scary" or "abstract" due to AN INCOMPLETE GRASP OF THE TRUE FULLNESS AND REALITY OF THE NATURE OF CONSCIOUSNESS.

I suppose that the most important aspect of this concept for contemporary societies is the realization that within each person is contained the Whole and they each can access this Wholeness (or more technically, return to conscious awareness of it).

Speak to the Innate or Primordial Nature.

If a lake "experiences" the fall of a twig from a tree into it, it has had an experience that does not change the nature of the lake. This is obvious; the twig merely rests happily on the surface of the lake and bobs merely along. The essence of the manifested stuff is this - IT IS HAPPENING ON THE SURFACE OF THE LAKE OF THE ABSOLUTE, as Itzhak Bentov has said. The lake, or your Innate Nature, remains unchanged by any experience had in manifested reality.

If the water in a glass spills into the lake, it is still the same and just as happy as when it was in the glass - it is not "different" or "changed." It is merely the GLASS which feels that there is something to lose or that something is changing. You are not the glass, as you know - fear things are of the glass and not the water. If you notice fear things in your mental field, my advice would be ignore them completely, they cannot harm you, especially if you SEE THEM FOR WHAT THEY ARE - of the Mind and not of the Innate Nature of Bliss and Light.

You are not the mind so to allow yourself to be controlled by it wastes energy as it tend to get caught in "circle thought" which will go around and around again. The way to eliminate "circle thought" is to LET GO OF IT ... when this occurs, the consciousness, which *knows what it is and is perfectly happy*, in no need of "protection," merely returns to that which it is essentially in "behind" the mind and emotions and body - Stillness expressing as Bliss, Love, Joy, etc.

Further commentary on Pure Consciousness?

Ah ... an endless topic! How can I emphasize how impossible it is from the vantage point of the Physical Plane to intellectually grasp anything but the merest hint of what the dynamics and essence of Pure Consciousness is? One could compare it to the fish swimming languidly and naturally in a bowl ... all FLOW ... effortless effort. When we consider the lifestyles of most Americans, we can see that they are mostly comprised of competition and striving. These dynamics are the polar opposites of the reality of Pure Consciousness.

When we examine this state described as Pure Consciousness, we can see that it can also be approached (from the ineffective perspective of the Physical Plane) as Pure Being. It doesn't take a rocket scientist to understand that in a condition of Pure Being there is NOTHING but Being ... there are no modifying qualities which are naturally associated with the condition of Manifestation. Now, it also is a very intuitive approach to recognize that in a Sea of Pure Consciousness there can be nothing to fear because it is merely UNSEPARATED CONSCIOUSNESS.

As has been discussed before, these concepts give you in physical incarnation no small degree of difficulty mainly because the LOWER MIND STARTS TO TRY TO CONCEPTUALIZE THE ESSENTIALLY NON-CONCEPTUAL. This point can't be stressed enough, because it is the source of much confusion and pure goofiness in your realm.

Speak again to individual reality as "condensation of consciousness."

Well, its as simple as it sounds ... All That Is, the Infinite, God, whatever you want to call the all-pervasive field of Pure Consciousness, chooses to actualize, for the purpose of experiences of varying kinds, DIFFERENT VIEWPOINTS with which to ultimately understand the essence of itself. You, and every other human being, are "condensations" (meaning alternately "accumulations") or "individualizations" of Pure Consciousness. This merely means that the single Reality is utilizing differing "windows" through which to view its manifestations for the purpose of comprehension, experience and understanding.

This simple dynamic causes no small measure of confusion, misunderstanding, fear, and general goofiness in your sphere as it is very difficult to grasp the operating dynamics of this relationship conceptually. That is, the intuitive knowledge that exists ubiquitously in the higher realms does not translate "downward" well and hence the great gobs of confusion and denial concerning this simple thing. This is the one thing that I would stress that is always of paramount importance: There is now, and never has been, nothing at all to worry about or be afraid of, because (say it with me now!) what can there possibly be to fear in Pure Consciousness, which by definition is merely BEING/EXISTENCE?

Something on the nature of condensed expressions of Pure Consciousness?

The nature of the condensed expression of Pure Consciousness is merely that it is COMPLETE OR WHOLE NOW. It resides in a Sea of Pure Wholeness of which it is a Whole part, or a *holographic "Mini - Wholeness."* The microcosm and macrocosm are mirrors of one another.

As one starts to ascend the ladder of Self-Realization, one will begin to OPEN more and more to that which they already are - Pure Consciousness, individualized and encapsulated in a nice neat form. The culmination of the Self-realization journey is COMPLETE WHOLENESS, nothing less. This complete Wholeness resides in the Sea of Complete Wholeness.

Address "according with" what is occurring in the physical world.

As it is the case that All That Is comprises a huge and complete Wholeness, and, of course by definition, NOTHING EXISTS OUTSIDE OF THIS WHOLENESS, then we can see that it is simply impossible for things to be any other way than right and groovy now! There are *no "bad" things, times, or experiences*; there is merely the failure to accord with what is occurring PERFECTLY in the Field of the Great Wholeness or Pure Consciousness or God, whichever you prefer.

This being the case, do this: ACCORD WITH WHAT IS HAPPENING NOW, and save yourself all sorts of heartache, striving, and just pure all-around goofiness. When one accords with what is happening, one comes first from a place of *observation*, to determine what is happening. Then one attempts to actualize a dynamic of "flowing with" whatever is occurring, even if this means leaving the circumstance, or "flowing on out." Nothing is ever, ever "going wrong" or "incorrectly" but instead all things always proceed perfectly!

The ability to accord with what is occurring allows one to be "in the flow" and REMOVES SUFFERING, to one degree or another.

Discuss the nature of individualized "specialization" or "life purpose."

If we consider that every essence of Pure consciousness is "designed" or "condensed" with certain EXPRESSIVE ASPECTS of All That Is, God, or Pure Consciousness, whichever you prefer, we can begin to understand that, hence, each condensed expression of Pure Consciousness will be UNIQUE, in some certain way. This is so Pure Consciousness, or YOU - there is no difference or separation, can have all sorts of *experiences* with which to understand itself and will be able to *express* certain specialized qualities or attributes. This remains as it always has been ... nothing has or is "changing" - IT THE SAME AS IT EVER WAS!! The only thing that is "changing" is: a) the daily reality of the manifested realms, and b) the individualized condensation's *awareness of what is already the case.*

More on one of my favorites - "relaxing into life"?

As has been discussed, relaxing into life is a very simple thing. It merely requires that the individualized unit of consciousness be PRESENT, ALERT, FOCUSED, AND CALM. In this condition, the person is then able to access increasing states of Being ... this very dynamic allows him to set aside negative energies such as fear, anger, jealousy, hate, etc. While in this state, he will be able to *perform more efficiently*, for everything becomes more FLOW-LIKE. It could be considered that one in the state of Flow is closer to the Original State of Being, and as such, less afflicted with the goofy concerns and illusions of the Physical Plane of existence.

When we examine those people who "succeed" in any endeavor in life, whether it merely is the ceaseless and excessive accumulation of money or some skill, we can detect that they, in some essential way, are coming from a place of more Being and efficiency. It could be said that those who are "struggling" are self-imposing this condition on their consciousness by ACCEPTING CONDITIONINGS that exist in the individual or group consciousness at this particular time. One should always "relax into" *any* place that one finds oneself as it will prove to be perfect at that point in time for the developmental needs of the individual.

Do not think that it is the case that every person will develop in a similar way ... certain "groups" of people will in a general sense, but everyone DEVELOPS IN A UNIQUE AND SPECIAL WAY. That is to say that certain general trends exist within "like groups," but in the end development remains very personal, special and wonderful.

Discuss the Form and the Formless.

Well, as you have noticed, the world (physical world) can be thought of as completely representational of what is occurring in Reality. If one looks up, the Sky ... Formless and Absolute, beyond change and modifying qualities (always the same). If one looks down, the world of Form ... solid, changeable, impermanent ... a cosmic dance of the Play of Consciousness. These two elements or factors represent additionally the polarity of Yin and Yang and can be thought of as occurring or springing from the Well of Pure Consciousness in its mode of manifestation.

There are times of manifestation and times of rest, or lack of manifestation. These, respectively, are called the Day of Brahman, and the Night of Brahman in the Hindu religion. If we can conceive of the simple fact that there is nothing but Pure Consciousness, then we can see that all circumstances are occurring within the Ocean of Pure Consciousness and are occurring as a Play of Experience, the purpose of which is the harvesting of experience and the expression of Joy/Love.

While it is true that many people will continue to perceive the world as a place of trial and tribulation, it can be seen that the world really is merely a PLAYGROUND OF EXPERIENCE and, since the Essential Nature of no human being is ever harmed by involvement in experience, then there is no reason not to RELAX INTO LIFE AND LIVE IT JOYOUSLY. It is only fear that causes the human unit of consciousness from doing this naturally.

Discuss the concept "All Creation is a Leela."

(The view of Creation as a Leela is one in which everything that is manifested is understood as the Play of the Infinite - that is, that the intention of manifestation is playful or sportive.)

Very good, wombat breath!! We can conceptualize the Dance of Consciousness as a Leela or CREATIVE MIND-PLAY OF THE INFINITE. This means that, much in the same way that an individualized expression of Pure Consciousness is creating their individualized world through use of the mind and its thought-forms, the infinite creates through the use of Cosmic Mind, during which Creating the "sparks" of itself - YOU HUMANS - are not harmed or changed by the experiences that are had in this great Cosmic Dream.

The world is an IDEA, essentially, and this should not cause fear because *it changes nothing at all* .... it's the same as it ever was!! You will find that if we flow with the knowledge that all of Creation is a Dance of Leela (in other words - it's just for fun, people!!) that life begins to unfold SIMPLY AND BEAUTIFULLY, with each person going toward what they are drawn to and providing service in this simple process.

So, if all of the manifested realms merely comprise a Leela, which could be considered a manifestation of FUN, one can merely choose to have FUN at any point in time since these are realms of FUN experience?

Well, Bucko, I would say that you're finally starting to grasp the tail end of this puppy!! There is now, and never has been, anything at all to be concerned with in the manifested realms as the individualized condensations of Pure Consciousness are SUPERIOR TO WHAT THEY PERCEIVE, as Roy Eugene Davis says.

We might liken this to a circumstance that is sometimes observed in daily life, that of the old man as he looks back upon his career. At a certain point in the reflection, if he is wise, he merely decides to accept his life in the way it occurred, peacefully, realizing that nothing can be done to alter it at this point.

So it is the same with the manifested realms ... they are FOR EXPERIENCE, NOTHING MORE, and so the condensed expressions of Pure Consciousness must merely learn to have fun in them!! There is no "harming" going on. There is no "struggle" going on. There are only "lessons" going on and once a person has passed a certain point of evolution they understand this completely and fully and then FALL INTO COMPLETE SERENITY, realizing that they are Immortals and not subject to any damage from the fun experiences that are happening here.

Everything is fun, there is no lack of fun, there is only the perception that pain and suffering exist by the lower mind, which has learned that things are scarce, lacking, non-flowing and generally not supportive. This learning is INCORRECT AND IS A CONDITIONING .... that is, something erroneously believed by the great masses of humanity.

As it is the case that humans are busily manufacturing their own realities, as you know, false or incorrect input merely causes them to Self-LIMIT. This is clearly understood by anyone that has a glimpse of how mind science operates. However, there is no need for limitation in a Swimming Sea of Pure Unlimitedness and this type of activity is merely SUFFERING with a capital "S," as well as ignorance.

Speak to the Joy that Dances in the Leela of manifestation!

What I would say is that THERE IS NOTHING THAT EXISTS THAT IS NOT PURE JOY!! Any other perspective is incorrect, or "illusory." The problem with manifested existence is the forgetting of this simple fact. How can a Light Being "Be" anything except pure Bliss? I would say that there is nothing to be concerned about in the "daily life" of human beings and most people are totally ignorant of this fact. If we consider that the manifested realms are DREAM-SCAPES or the LEELA (COSMIC PLAY) of the Infinite, we can see that no harm is occurring to the individualized condensations of Pure Consciousness, although most times they are completely unaware of this.

But merely do this: view the Play of Consciousness as fun incarnate (or Fun in Motion), and live your life as if All is Fun. In other words, ACCORD WITH THE FUN THAT ALREADY EXISTS, and you will find that your life becomes full of Love and Fun and Joy and Bliss. There is never any reason to do otherwise, it is merely *ignorance* that is causing most humans to deny (or not acknowledge) their spiritual nature.

More thoughts on the Whole and Wholeness?

If we consider that All That Is constitutes a Great and Complete Wholeness, we can see that THERE CAN BE NOTHING THAT LIES OUTSIDE OF THIS WHOLENESS and all perceived "negative" or "bad" things are merely incorrect conclusions based on *lack of information* and so, as we've discussed, everything is RIGHT AND PERFECT and there are no "imperfect" things AT ALL, anywhere. The nature of this lack of information lies in the *essential energetic relationships* of All That Is.

We can see that many people are going about the laborious process of trying to change the world into a Paradise externally, but this is unnecessary, as *it is already a Paradise, here and now, and always has been.* As there exists nothing but an Oceanic Expanse of Love and Joy, in which human beings are immersed like little corks in the sea, bobbing around, the experiences which are occurring as we speak in the Physical Plane of existence are occurring for the expressed use and growth of the individualized unit of Pure Consciousness.

When, after many trials and tribulations, covering the span of many incarnated lifetimes, the individual finally becomes aware of their True Nature, they can easily see the nature and purpose of physical manifestation and so it no longer troubles them in the least, I can assure you. When we consider that many people are slowly coming awake at this point in time due to their own efforts and the pervasive force of higher consciousness because of the approaching Great Moment of Stillness, we can see that this is truly a wonderful time to exist in physical incarnation. Do not be concerned with anything at all, for what can harm a unit of Pure Consciousness?

The Buddhists seem to view the Physical Plane as "suffering," but if Joy pervades all, is it not true that Paradise is everywhere?

Ah ... very good point! The Buddhists are engaged in the practice of a RELIGION and as such, must rely on information that, although very good in many respects, was disseminated a very long time ago for the conditions and circumstances present *at that time.* While it could be said that there still exists "suffering" in the world, and that they have in hand many, many useful concepts to help ease the suffering, WHAT IS ONE MAN'S SUFFERING IS ANOTHER MAN'S PARADISE.

You might find that since it is true that Joy pervades all, that Paradise is, of course, everywhere, and that it is merely certain distractions of the mental and emotional bodies that are preventing the huge body of mankind access to this Ocean of internal/external Joy. From the perspective of those such as yourself who operate outside of established religious constructs, it could be said that all currently extant religions have something to offer humanity, but that in the end one should merely take from each that which "makes sense" and discard the rest. This is a simple and fundamental law of manifestation because there are many different "windows" through which to view the single Reality and one wouldn't want ANY OF THESE WINDOWS TO GET DIRTY OR BROKEN!

Speak more to suffering as this is a universal problem for humans.

As there is nothing at all to worry about, and never has been, one could say that the OVER-ACTIVITY OF THE MIND, in terms of trying to analyze personal circumstances (i.e. family things, stuff at work, the Meaning of Life), merely causes suffering, like the Buddha said. This is because the lower mind is designed as the *instrument of individualized separation for the purpose of experience gathering.* That is, the lower mind's purpose is to identify and specialize things.

But here is the big problem ... the things of the higher spiritual realms cannot be understood with the lower mind as it is LIMITED, NOT UNLIMITED. So it merely "contracts" in a fear-defensive mode if it perceives something which is exponentially beyond it's grasp. It must merely be *relaxed* enough to allow the higher things to be experienced.

Worry is the single most energy draining dynamic facing the body of humanity today. It serves no useful purpose and merely causes the individual to become needlessly tired and energy depleted.

Speak again on Simplicity.

As has been stated, everything is already simple because EVERYTHING IS SIMPLY CONSCIOUSNESS. It is merely the *lack of ability to accord with simplicity* that is sort of mucking up the entire works. If we have a situation in which two people are approaching a problem and one says: "I think I'll make it simple," then this one will usually come up with a good, direct solution in a short amount of time. If the other person likes things complicated, he will come up with some intense, goopy mess based on his own ego needs.

If we think of Simplicity like a walnut lying on the ground under the tree, we can see that Mr. Walnut does nothing but lie there, passively, until acted upon. Let's say Mr. Squirrel comes along and picks up the walnut and eats it. The walnut does not bemoan it's fate in life ... "Oh how horrible, to be eaten by a squirrel!" ... it merely "goes with the flow," as this is The Way of Nature.

Since today is Independence Day, any more thoughts on Freedom?

Well, well, well ... very good question! As you know, the essence of Freedom is Simplicity and the essence of Simplicity is Freedom, it's kind of a two way street! You will find that the aspect of consciousness known in your realm as freedom is, once again, merely an *innate quality inherent in the original nature* of the individualized condensations of Pure Consciousness and, as such, CANNOT BE DEPLETED, REMOVED, OR ALTERED from its original condition in any way.

This means that everyone is always free and it is merely the lack of understanding of the nature of this freedom that causes people to believe that they are in chains. The nature of this is Freedom is COMPLETE AND TOTAL, UNBOUNDED ... so that if one will merely try to conceptualize what this means, one will be able to begin to apply the reality of total Freedom to their earth-life. It is the realization that one is FREE NOW that generates the greatest "personal sense" of Freedom, as you might suspect.

If a person is an Immortal energy being that cannot be killed or harmed in any way, then there is nothing to fear at all!! Fearlessness is Freedom, or to put it another way ... LOVE IS FREEDOM. If an individual will merely accept the all, as it is, unconditionally, then they are free now because they feel no need to CHANGE ANYTHING. What this means is that they are now, and will continue to be, swimming in a Sea of Pure Bliss and Consciousness of which they are a blissful part. They are Bliss right now, not later!! This means that they can know the level of their own Freedom by merely understanding that it exists now and they need do nothing at all to "earn" it!! To put this another way, NOTHING THAT IS DONE ALTERS THE STATE OF THEIR INNATE NATURE AND FREEDOM!!

So, it is true that since one, at an Essential Level, is already completely free, one can merely try to "relax into" or live from this already extant state of freedom?

Well, Mark, it looks like you've hit the nail on the head on that one ... it is merely the mistaken assumption that one has to DO SOMETHING that is restraining and constricting the body of humanity in the experience of their Innate Freedom. There is no need to DO anything as there is nothing to be done; *freedom is an already extant state.*

So, yes, it is true that one merely makes the decision to live from this already Free Essence and one finds that things immediately begin to go and flow much better for them. Freedom is the complete realization that there is nothing at all to be done to "earn" freedom, you are ALREADY FREE!

The problems, ailments, and circumstances that happen or occur to the body and personality are non-injurious to the Original Essential Nature of all human units of consciousness. It could be said that one is free to walk through life secure in the knowledge that no event or events can injure them essentially in any way. If this is true, what can there EVER be to be concerned or overly worried about?

Whip some more on me regarding the Great Wholeness!

Oh, so we're feeling adventurous today, eh? What one could say, once again, is that the Great Wholeness is a concept and, as such, is very helpful but not the same as the experiential result of EXPERIENCING THE NATURE OF THE GREAT WHOLENESS. The Great Wholeness is individual Wholeness. The Great Wholeness is collective Wholeness. The Great Wholeness is Wholeness period!!

As it is the case that there is nothing at all separate from this Wholeness, we can see that there can be nothing at all to fear or be concerned with. This is why the advanced yogis of all lands are Blissful, chuckling fun-pots ... they know that everything is Pure Grooviness and so they merely Groove with it All.

Consequently, we can see that, as one develops their vehicles of consciousness, one will always enter a place of more and more Innateness which includes all of the various Innate Qualities like Bliss, Joy, Love, etc. One will eventually reach a place where they are in complete control of their consciousness, or to put it another way, their consciousness remains COMPLETE OR WHOLE in any manifested realm. They are able to perceive the energetic underpinnings occurring in all of the manifested realms.

Think of it all simply, like this: the Wholeness that you are TRANSCENDS the body/mind ... the Wholeness that you are EMBRACES the body/mind!

Any more thoughts on consciousness?

If one can view the Endless Sea of Consciousness that pervades All in light of the intrinsic essence of Reality, then one can clearly see that All Is One and there is no possibility that there can be anything "wrong" or "bad," there can only be PERFECTION in varying degrees of realization by the numberless individualized condensations of consciousness, or human beings. You will find that consciousness is the thing, so to speak, and it will be the buzz word of the near future only because many more people will realize the importance of this perspective, as will the scientific community.

The wonderful Secret of the Ages is that everyone *already has all that they need* as a part of their original Innate consciousness and nothing is required but to realize this, as it is in the Realization of an ALREADY EXTANT STATE that the Freedom comes.

The Great Moment of Stillness

"But the soul that moves in the world of
the senses and yet keeps the senses in
harmony, free from attraction and
aversion, finds rest in quietness."
Bhagavad Gita 2, 64

Now we come to what may be one of the most talked about and hotly debated topics ... the Big Millennial Event. This, too, has been called by many names and foretold by various prophets and predicted as occurring on various dates around the year 2000. Although my channeling efforts have produced a specific date, I feel that it is the entire process of the expansion of Higher Consciousness that is the important focal point, the rest will merely take care of itself. This event will be fundamentally "consciousness raising" in nature and will affect everyone. There is no reason for any fear concerning this event, for what can there be to fear in Pure Consciousness? Very possibly many people will experience a dramatic shift in their way of life and viewpoint of Reality. Old methods of operation based in fear may be ineffective ... previous successful behaviors based in "struggle" may prove unsuccessful.

This process and event, from my information, has a physical, scientific connection that has to do with the position regionally of our galaxy in relation to a "torus-type" (see Itzhak Bentov's **Stalking The Wild Pendulum**) or expansion/contraction model of our manifested Universe. The event naturally occurs in the region where galaxies reach the point of Stillness between the "expansion" phase and the returning "contraction" phase of the manifested Universe. A good model of this would be when one throws a ball in the air, the point where it "hangs" before returning Earthward would be analogous to this rest moment, or Great Moment of Stillness. Stillness is naturally associated with expansion of Consciousness.

Once again, there are many different lenses to view this event through. Without further commentary, I offer up the channeled information, as it speaks for itself.

Is the information regarding the "rest moment" of the universe in **The Starseed Transmissions** (by Ken Carey) correct and on what date will this occur?

Yes, indeed, the information presented in **The Starseed Transmissions** is correct in regard to the upcoming "rest moment." This can best be conceptualized as an event that will fundamentally change the energetic relationships in your sphere. Although it is true that it will be the cause of great upheaval, the essence of *any* change in the physical realm is that it does not harm the human units of consciousness essentially. The Christian perspective is somewhat hung up in oppositional terms such as "life" and "death" and these are merely employed to designate the continuance or non-continuance of the PHYSICAL FORM.

You will find that many, many people are very confused on this upcoming shift, for no good reason, as it is merely a NATURALLY OCCURRING "SCIENTIFIC" DYNAMIC that becomes manifest at the rest point of expansion/contraction in the life of any manifested universe. The nature of the energetic shift that will occur is this: during the "rest moment," the vibrational dynamic of THE UNIVERSE will be quiescent. As you know from meditation, contact with higher levels of consciousness occurs when things are stilled in the Physical Plane.

During this period of time there will be a great infusion of "higher consciousness," "higher energy," or whatever term the individual chooses to describe the Infinite All That Is. I can assure you that this will not be an occasion for fear of any kind, and the Christian perspective often merely causes unnecessary fears regarding and revolving around this question: "what's gonna happen to ME?" The Unity of Consciousness is a fact of nature at all times, so this event will merely make this fact known, THROUGH DIRECT EXPERIENCE, to more incarnate human beings.

As far as terminology utilized, **The Starseed Transmissions** utilizes a Christian lens to view this occurrence because the leanings of the author are best described as Christian, however the important points contained within this upcoming occurrence are:

1. The nature of consciousness as experienced by the ordinary human unit of consciousness will shift dramatically upward.

2. The experience of time in your realm will change in this manner: the essence of "time," as you know, is that there is ultimately no linear time, this is merely the unfoldment of events is a sequential manner as experienced in your realm. From this point onward, people will be aware that there is only the "now" and that all measures of linear time exist merely for the sake of EXPERIENCE IN THE PHYSICAL PLANE. It could be said that this knowledge is already present in the higher consciousness of each individualized unit of consciousness and so it is only the eruption of this into the "waking" consciousness that will change.

3. Those that are engaged in energy dynamics that might be termed controlled by and generated from fear will find that their world is gone ... i.e. the use of fear over others is not effective, the use of fear as a protective tool for survival is not effective, and generally, the whole "fear" dynamic will fall by the wayside because THERE WILL SIMPLY BE NO NEED FOR THE UTILIZATION OF IT. Now, there are those that will find this change somewhat, shall we say, unacceptable, and these persons will generate their own extremely difficult period of adjustment. In the end, this may result in their "death" of form on the Physical Plane BUT THIS DOES NOT MEAN THAT THEY "DIE." They will merely continue to exist, simply in differing realms of consciousness.

What is the date when this will occur?

This will occur on December 25, 2012.

Will the Great Moment of Stillness occur in just one region of this manifested Universe or universally?

Since we can consider Itzhak Bentov's model of the universe to be fairly accurate, the Great Moment of Stillness will occur in one *region* on your side of the torus continuously, with different galaxies, stars and the associated smaller units of consciousness passing through this region as they arrive at the region. While we can see that they will then pass "out the other side" and continue travel in the outer rim of the torus, the essential nature of perceptual abilities in regard to levels of consciousness will be altered, as previously discussed, by the experience of the Moment of Stillness and the attendant expansion of time and consciousness.

If we can conceptualize the expansion of time as the cessation of movement and the experience of the Eternal Now, then we can see that this "moment" will NOT BE BOUND BY "OBJECTIVE" TIME and will be experienced subjectively by the individualized units of consciousness in different ways, some perceiving it to be "long," some perceiving it to be "short." Since this is merely a *naturally occurring dynamic* in all manifested universes, there is nothing to be concerned with or afraid of and the experience will prove to be wonderful and fascinating when extracted from the overlain fear element. Do not think that there will be anything to be concerned with, as this will be a quite wonderful thing.

Please describe just what the heck is going on in the Physical Plane at this time.

One can view the Physical Plane, as you know, as a realm of experience. It is the case that at this particular point in time the reality of the Physical Plane, which, once again, is generated and maintained by the collective consciousness of the entities incarnate IN the Physical Plane, is such that we can view things as in a period of EXTREMELY RAPID CHANGE energy-wise. The ways of the past, once so reliable and opportune, will now prove to be ineffective to a greater or lesser degree and individuals will find that it is only by "according with the Tao" or "going with the flow" that they make progress in "personal" goals and doings.

If we view the Physical Plane as it truly is, merely an energy (or consciousness) CONSTRUCT, we can see that it is impossible to understand just what the heck is going on unless one has developed their own level of consciousness to the degree that they can directly perceive what is happening, energy-wise. So, we can see that for a very few entities incarnate at this particular point in time, this period will be one of acceptance and understanding ... however, for most people it will be a time that can be characterized by the very phrase ... "just what the heck is going on here?"

We can say that many people will find themselves without jobs as they age, always scary; they will find themselves in jobs "beneath their qualifications" and they will find themselves in various "negative" and detrimental circumstances which would also include health-related things, family-related things, "life-choice" related things, etc. Do not think that this time will be easy for those incarnate in the Physical Plane! While it is true that it will not necessarily be "hard," it could best be said that it will merely be DIFFERENT. Those who try to "control" or "struggle" too much in certain areas of their lives may find that these areas remain unfulfilling. You will see that those who "go with the flow" will find new avenues of expression, income, love, and life that they may not have even CONCEIVED OF prior to this new shift in consciousness.

I am aware that it may take many people quite some time to come around to this way of "Being" but it will eventually become apparent that this is the "way of the future," so to speak. When it becomes apparent that one cannot get along so readily utilizing the "old" methods ... many more people will become open to the new.

Discuss the Light of Pure Consciousness and how it is perceived by the human unit of consciousness.

Well, what we could say about the Light of Pure Consciousness is that it's Everywhere, it's Everywhere! When one has refined the cerebrospinal system to the degree that one can begin to access higher states of consciousness, the following things usually occur: 1) perception of energy flows throughout the body in various locales and especially at the energy centers called by the Indian metaphysicians "chakras," 2) illumination of the various vehicles of consciousness in such a way that the individual will be able to utilize them to access the specific frequencies or "aspects" of consciousness that they represent, 3) continued unfoldment of the ENTIRE energetic system until such time that the individualized unit of consciousness will perceive, in one of many ways, that

EVERYTHING IS MERELY CONSCIOUSNESS ... there is nothing else.

What we might consider the Light of Pure Consciousness can be described in this way .... it's Bright, and it's White, and it's Everywhere, man! What I mean is this ... those that perceive the Light of God (or whatever name) will see it everywhere, FLOWING WHITENESS in everything, making the individualized essence of consciousness completely sure of the interconnected nature of All That Is. Now, as to the individual perception of the Light of Oneness, we would have to say that this perception remains *individual* ... each will see it in the (surprise) PERFECT way for them.

As we come closer to what we have been calling the Great Moment of Stillness (once again, merely a naturally occurring dynamic and nothing to be afraid of) more and more people will "wake up" to their own Original Nature as individualized units of the One Reality - Supreme or Pure Consciousness (God). Just because there are those who would say that there is but ONE way to attain the realization of Oneness, it is necessary to attempt, at this time, to "spread the word," so to speak, that there are MANY paths that all lead to the same place and the individualized units of consciousness should merely *seek those ways, things, and practices* which "feel right" to them and provide the easiest and most joyful awakening.

This does not have to be hard, and, in fact, since everything is simple, we can see that it is important to approach this from a SIMPLE AND RELAXED perspective on an individual basis. No struggle! No pain! No fighting! Just relaxation!

Speak more to cerebrospinal refinement?

The refinement of the cerebrospinal system, culminating in Self-Realization, is the entire purpose of incarnation in the earth-realm. Therefore, if an individual works diligently toward this goal then he merely effectively raises his ENERGY INTERFACE WITH THE MANIFESTED UNIVERSE IN WHICH HE LIVES ... i.e., the Universe will function in such a way as to "co-operate" in greater and greater ways with such an individual.

There are certain aspects of this process that take awhile to manifest or, to use another manner of speech, there is some "catching up" that gets done by the individual's various bodies or vehicles of consciousness energetically. As it is true that you are, at this moment, living and immersed in a Sea of Joy at all times, it is also true that attempting to find or discover those things that give you Joy will lead you to a better place of incarnated existence since you are then merely simplifying your life and *going to what your are drawn to*.

Money, in any appreciable quantity, only comes when one goes to what one is drawn to. If we consider that the bulk of humanity is going about doing that which they were told to do by one unit of consciousness or another, we can see that this is one of the major reasons that YOUR REALM IS IN A STATE OF DEEP CRISIS. People have managed to mess up the natural simplicity that is simply their birthright.

The various disciplines that you are involved with are methods and ways for many people to return to simplicity and flow, as you are well aware. The upcoming times will only be difficult for those who *will not adapt to the great changes that are headed your way*. The Great Moment of Stillness will expand the essence of your reality so that those who are completely unevolved will be able to perceive the various aspects of Higher Consciousness. This, as has been mentioned, will not be pleasant only for those who allow themselves to be caught up in unnecessary fear, as all fear, by definition, is. What is there to fear in a rippling sea of Pure Bliss?

Speak to the various physical manifestations that may begin to occur at this Millennial time ... it seems to me now that these are merely attempts to re-establish harmony and balance. Can you go into the specific energy or consciousness mechanics involved?

Well, Mark, just "what the heck is going on" as you would put it is a simple thing. The Earth, a highly evolved consciousness in its own right, has reached a place of imbalance due to the activities of its most highly evolved inhabitants - human beings. As it is true that *every manifested system attempts to achieve harmony and then remain in balance*, we can see that ol' Mother Earth is merely going about trying to re-establish equilibrium.

Now, much in the same way that the re-establishment of equilibrium in an individualized expression of consciousness causes that not-so-wonderful experience of "dense vibration" at times, the same is true for energetic dynamics occurring on a larger scale. As you live in a realm of VIBRATION, balancing of the Yin-Yang components requires ACTIVITY (as in the individual with the movement of the breath or T'ai Chi) and this is why the expression of this self-balancing consists of storms, earth movements, oceanic movements and changes, etc.

The manifested reality in your realm, i.e. the "daily life" which everyone is experiencing, is being generated by the *mass consciousness of the summed humans in incarnation.* This means that whatever pervasive thought forms exist in the mass consciousness will manifest YOUR OWN REALITY FOR YOU. As it is the case that everything is now in the process of "balancing out" because of the slowing of the entire galaxy as you near the Great Moment of Stillness, we can see that there will most likely be quite a bit of "dense vibration" worldwide over the course of the time between now and 2012.

This does not mean that human beings can "do nothing" or are powerless in this circumstance ... they can easily start to change their relationship with the Earth and their own manifested reality by RAISING THE LEVEL OF THEIR INDIVIDUALIZED CONSCIOUSNESS. It is observable in your world society that this is not occurring at a rapid rate, so it is my opinion that there will indeed be quite some dynamic of "dense vibration" ... floods, strange weather, oceanic and land movements, etc. These are merely attempts by the Earth to balance out unresolved energetic dynamics and should be not viewed in any other way ... i.e. Judgments, Apocalypses, Gloom and Doom and the like.

As the Innate Essence of each individualized expression of Pure Consciousness is, right now, as we speak, completely *free, alive, Immortal, and blissfully happy and content*, we can see that these things, once again, are merely experiences for consciousness units, meaning YOU. This is one of the aspects of the message that you can "get out" that will be of the most help to a large range and variety of people ... they are NON-PHYSICAL BEINGS and the things that are occurring in this realm can hurt them no more than a fly is harmed by the crazed attempts of an angry homeowner to do him in by wildly swinging a baseball bat.

What observations do you have on the various "millennial events" predicted in Gordon-Michael Scallion's book **Notes from the Cosmos**?

What I would say, Mark, is that basically, the information is very good, with the qualifier that, like other channeled information dealing with PROBABLE FUTURES, the very field of dynamic energy that is being forecast about is going about change based on the actions of the elements or units of consciousness within that field. However, this being said, I would add that it is true that there is going to be a great dynamic of dense vibration in regard to the cleansing and balancing activites that will be occurring with the earth, starting in 1998, as he says. This means this ... because certain "better" probable futures were not selected by the mass consciousness of humanity, then what we will see is a dynamic of INTENSE EARTH CHANGES, caused merely by the attempts of the "Mother Planet" to energetically balance itself, which it must do in preparation for the Great Moment of Stillness. Now, although Scallion does not mention the Great Moment Of Stillness, this does not change the fact that IT IS COMING! The information that an individual gains access to and/or decides to distribute will be perfect for them and those that are drawn to their teachings and ways. You will find that if you merely OBSERVE what is occurring in the natural world, there will be many signs of great change and this includes (but may not be limited to):

1. THE MELTING OF THE POLAR ICE. Here we have it .. the great "sweat down/melt down"! The polar ice caps are *now*, not later, undergoing a dynamic of slow melting (see the references in the back of Scallion's book regarding the already dissolved platforms of ice). As this slow melting intensifies, we will see a corresponding rise in the world's oceans which will *directly, though relatively slowly, impact the land masses of the world.*

2. LOOK TO THE SKIES! It will be discovered that there is a newly approaching star, termed by Scallion "the Blue Star," which will be captured by the gravitational dynamics present in the solar system. This will lead to the formation of a double or binary star system with the current sun. This is, of course, an observable astronomical process and the astronomers are the ones that will first detect it. Many people will be surprised by the Blue Star's arrival, most probably later this year (1998). The Blue Star can be conceptualized as a mass of HIGH CONSCIOUSNESS ENERGY, or to put it in Scallion's language, a collection of heavenly beings. It's purpose is to merely add a HIGH VIBRATIONAL ESSENCE OR GUIDE-FORCE to the already extant "astrological" dynamic of the solar system. In this way, it can be considered to resonate with the soul energy level of existence.

3. There will be seen MUCH, MUCH EXTREME WEATHER, including storms, hurricanes, tornadoes, very high winds and all sorts of other "displaced" or evolving weather patterns. This, once again, is due to the balancing activities of the Yin-Yang components of the earth, a high consciousness in its own right. This balancing activity merely requires MOTION and hence we have the motion of the wind, sea and earth in response.

4. There will also be a huge increase in the number of EARTH QUAKES AND EARTH MOVEMENTS, for the reasons mentioned above. This will cause great economic distress and it would not be advisable to *live in earthquake prone areas!!* Visiting them is another matter and should not necessarily be avoided for short periods of time. All of these changes, and especially the RISING WATER will be seen to take some time and not happen suddenly (with the noticeable exception of intense weather and earthquakes, of course).

5. It could be said that there will be found to be occurring a greater and greater number of HUMAN CONFLICTS, on a more extended nature, symptomatically indicated in the present by the *ongoing polarity of fear vs. love* that is occurring in groups, communities and nations. This will most probably, unfortunately,

include MAJOR WARS, which will be centered in the Middle East and Europe and which will not directly affect the U.S., although, of course, all wars affect everyone on the planet. This will escalate until the unusual and pervasive nature of the ongoing earth changes forces the participants to realize that they do not have the time or energy to be engaged in this goofiness over lands that are RAPIDLY DISAPPEARING! This dynamic, unfortunately, has progressed a bit too far at this time to be subject to reversal by actions taken at the current level of human consciousness.

6. If we consider that there will be major ECONOMIC DISASTERS that occur due to the increased stress on the social systems of major earth changes, coupled with the strange goofiness of warring over possession of lands, we can see that almost no segment of the human population will get away without great hardship. Those in the U.S. will fair the best, due to the isolation of the country from the areas of war and the excellent economy when compared with the rest of the world, but it will be very different here than in the "Reagan 80's." You can count on that!

Do you agree with Scallion's observations concerning life on Mars and Venus?

Yes, completely. In the distant past, there was a race of proto-beings (physical) on Mars and there exist today life forms in the astral and higher realms on Mars and Venus. Venus, being far too hostile of an environment, has never supported life in the physical.

What about Scallion's description of the Great Pyramid and its operation?

Once again, this is basically good, although I would describe the Great Pyramid, as are many, many other pyramids on this planet and others, to be a FOCUSING, RESONANT DEVICE, the purpose of which is the resonant attunement to higher or different levels of consciousness. The Great Pyramid works like this: a "priest," or someone with esoteric knowledge of higher consciousness, as well as scientific knowledge of *vibration and resonance,* would utilize the Great Pyramid, a highly tuned RESONANT MACHINE OR INSTRUMENT, to assist in accessing higher states of consciousness - which can be understood to be merely *higher vibrational states of existence.* That is, everything is vibration, as you know, so if one merely comes into RESONANT ATTUNEMENT WITH THESE VIBRATIONS (hence the Guru-Chela relationship), one can experience, to the degree that their cerebrospinal system is evolved and attuned also, the states of consciousness present.

It could be said that merely exposure to the high vibrations (as in exposure to high vibrations during darshan or other personal encounters with dynamic higher consciousness energy) will set into motion those physical and etheric processes necessary to refine the cerebrospinal system. So, the pyramids can be considered to be BIG VIBRATING ATTUNEMENT CHAMBERS, whose characteristic shape, the shape and size of the various internal chambers, and the geographic location in relation to known Earthean sources of energy are all big and important factors.

Pyramids are easy and simple, they are made of TRIANGLES, get it?, as well as being constructed of materials that are beneficial to concentrating and focusing the cosmic energies. After they are collected and focused, they can be attuned to by resonant interface utilizing the specifically tuned chambers, crystals, and other tuning devices (gasses, etc.) present as a part of the working structure of the pyramid.

Everyone seems tired, not just me but lots of people ... just what the heck is going on?

If we consider that the Physical Plane of existence is being infused with a higher and higher concentration of "High Consciousness" energy on a DAILY basis, due to the fact that the galaxy is becoming regionally closer to the "Spot of Stillness," then we can see that, not only is the Earth demonstrating "dense vibration" in the form of balancing activities that include weird weather, storms, etc., but PEOPLE WILL EXPERIENCE PERSONALIZED CIRCUMSTANCES that could best be described as rapid evolution of Consciousness or "intense energy work."

When there is no time for the individualized unit of Consciousness to allow the energy that is increasingly flowing through each consciousness unit to balance in terms of the individual's energetic system, the individual will feel tired and "sluggish." The ideal condition during this time would be one of little or no stress and tension, the accumulation of which merely NEGATIVELY AFFECTS THE MASS CONSCIOUSNESS. As it is the case that not much can be immediately done concerning the chosen lifestyles of most of the incarnated humans at this time, then each person will be left to attempt to work out these energy concerns on their own or in small groups.

This is a rather ineffective manner of dealing with such great daily changes in the energy/consciousness present in your sphere, and many people will not generally attain the *degree of relaxation required* to allow these energetic dynamics to balance and harmonize throughout the individual's energy bodies. As has been said, this means that everyone is in "for a bumpy ride" but this, of course, only affects the individual's expression in the Physical Plane of existence. If we consider that these times are times of great change for everyone now in incarnation, we can see that there will be various periods during which one may feel that things are unfolding "too rapidly" or in an "out of control" manner but, of course, and I must stress this, *things are always occurring perfectly in all of the manifested realms.*

If one will try to accept this as a reality, then it will allow the individualized expression of Pure Consciousness to not fight against the FLOW of what is occurring but instead ride in the current of the flow. Once again, this is a simple thing ... everything is essentially simple and it is merely the resistance to or ignorance of this Simplicity that causes no end of pain and suffering in the material realms. As it is the case that things at this time are changing in the direction of GREATER MANIFESTATION OR AWARENESS OF HIGHER CONSCIOUSNESS, then we can view the overall change as "good" or "more natural," although on an individual level there will be times when it will be temporarily difficult or strange. One must merely "ride the bucking bronco of Consciousness" to end up in a wonderful place of more Being.

Speak more on the topic of Simplicity?

As it is the case that there is nothing to the entire construct of the manifested realms except simplicity, we could say that simplicity is merely the Natural Order of all things. There is no complexity at all, complex things are simply the EXPRESSION OF SIMPLICITY.

Where all the goofiness and problems begin is when the human unit of Pure Consciousness starts to mistakenly believe that the MENTAL ANALYSIS of the events and occurrences that are taking place in the Physical Plane of existence will lead them to a place of understanding. This is to say that mental analysis can be productive and helpful for many things but *all transcendent realization and understanding is done at the intuitive level* and not through the use of the rational mind, which, as we've discussed, is limited.

There is not now, and never has been, any reason for the condensed expression of Pure Consciousness to engage in over-analytical thought because it does not lead to the expected conclusion of *resolution,* but instead merely leads to a place of *suffering.* It is through BEING that the human being learns to reach a place that IS FOR HIM and that he loves, laughing out loud at the shear FUN OF LIFE.

If we consider that most people do not understand that Simplicity is Everywhere, and mistakenly believe that Complexity will provide the answers to pervasive problems of the Physical Plane, then we can see why so many people's lives in incarnation are in chaos. They are trying to approach the "good life" from the wrong end, and need only RELAX AND ENJOY THEMSELVES instead of striving, striving, striving with every little thing. Accessing the Oceans and Oceans of Bliss and Joy that exist everywhere right now merely requires a RELAXED MENTAL FRAMEWORK, which provides a base of STILLED EMOTIONS and allows Innate Joy to shine, shine on down through.

This cannot be stressed enough in your realm because the individualized condensations of Pure Consciousness are not open to this information due to extreme and pervasive cultural conditioning. You would do well to convince everyone you know that FUN, RELAXATION AND ENJOYMENT is the way to attain a state of flow in the shortest amount of time.

How is a person to make money in these changing times?

The essence of all this money stuff is simple, as you are beginning to see, one merely does what they are DRAWN TO and the MONEY FOLLOWS. This is merely the way things work in the Physical Plane of existence ... no big deal! Yet it is a wonderful deal once the individualized expression of consciousness gets a handle on this sucker!! With a certain fullness of time you will see, as you are seeing more and more each day, that everything boils down to Simplicity and *relaxation is the gateway to this Simplicity on every level of existence.* No pain, no struggle, no fighting!

As each individualized unit of Pure Consciousness makes its way back to the place of consciousness wherein it can determine the elemental nature of Reality for itself, there are many wonderful events and experiences to be had and ENJOYED. There is only experience in the manifested realms, nothing else. Some of these experiences may be pleasant, some may not, but none of them harm the essence of the individual, WHICH IS SPIRIT, ENERGY OR CONSCIOUSNESS, WHICHEVER YOU PREFER.

So, in regards to the "money thang," all that is necessary is to find *what you love* and do that. Although this does not seem to make rational sense, you are then "taken care of" by the Universe, which is merely ANOTHER PART OF YOU, as you know. YOU ARE SWIMMING IN A SEA OF YOURSELF, so does it not make sense that you would want to support yourself? I thought so!!

So, don't wait for the money to come before you enjoy yourself and do what you love - do so now and the money will come?

Very good, Bucko!! As you know, essentially NOTHING IS REQUIRED of the condensed expressions of Pure Consciousness as they are all SELF-COMPLETE NOW. This means that once the individual Realizes this, they will automatically act in such a way that they DRAW prosperity to them because they are Whole now - that is, they don't "need" the money to "feel good" or actualize any place of Being.

There is always abundance, as it is the basic nature of the Great Wholeness - IT IS WHOLE OR COMPLETE, get it? This means It, and Its aspects, do not "need" anything. When "needing" is released, then grooviness and FUN can begin or be maximized.

How about a perennial favorite, relaxing into life?

OK, consider this - all of a person's personal stuff always works itself out through linear time and that's the whole point - don't sweat the SMALL stuff, don't sweat the BIG stuff, don't sweat ANY stuff at all 'cause *it is all merely experience or the Play of Consciousness,* none of which harms one minute speck of the Essential Nature of the human unit of Pure Consciousness.

Relaxing into life might be considered to be as easy as eating a huge warm piece of apple pie a la mode ... it's warm and tasty and sweet and yummy and you like it so you want more and you don't like bitter goopy sea urchin sushi so why are you eating it and not the yummy apple pie? Every day of the year people are engaged in performing jobs they don't like, dealing with circumstances they are not drawn to when what is necessary to do is to *go toward what you are drawn to* and then *relax into it and enjoy it.* IT'S SIMPLE, IT'S EASY, IT'S FUN!!

More information on individual energy interface with the Universe?

As was stated earlier, when the individual begins to progress spiritually, THROUGH LARGELY HIS OWN EFFORTS (with some Grace thrown in), he will find that many things merely "fall in his lap" or come easily. This is because he has increased his energy or consciousness interface with the Universe and can utilize this new range of power, if he knows how.

The how is fairly simple and, although things will come if no effort at all is exerted, it is mainly a combination of INTENTION AND DESIRE. Merely be open to the various possibilities and they will present themselves in a multitude of manners. We can view this process like the one in operation if a student has done well and merely *learned how to use the tools which have always been at hand.*

Each condensed expression of Pure Consciousness is a free being and always has been, so one always has the ability to choose whatever path they desire to take at any point in time. FREEDOM IS

THE INHERENT STATE OF EXISTENCE, and, as such, it is only right and natural that individuals desire freedom of one sort or another. If we consider that most people are shackled behind the most obstructive self-imposed limits, then we can see that each person who is able to progress spiritually is greatly assisting the others, both by raising the level of mass consciousness by his actions (kriyas) alone, and by direct contact with various individuals during which he will naturally want to share information and techniques which have allowed him to discover Bliss, Joy, Love ... you know the list.

Why is this so is simple? IT IS MERELY THE WAY THAT THE MANIFESTED REALMS OPERATE; there is no other fundamental reason. We may also view this as previously described: the individual merely follows his Bliss, his Joy, or what he is drawn to naturally, and things just work out.

Any more thoughts on Joy?

It's everywhere, it's everywhere!! In the Dancing Ocean of Consciousness, Joy is the all-pervasive EXPRESSION of manifested consciousness ... it is a Joy to be alive or to exist (the Joy of Pure Being), it is a Joy to celebrate this existence, and it is a JOY to share this knowledge with those that may be struggling with the absence or lack of knowledge. *Joy is merely all there is, there is nothing else at all!!*

Sudden realizations of this simple fact, in one form or another, are called Satori or Enlightenment experiences (as you know, this can also be expressed as wisdom, love, peace, bliss, truth, etc.). The trouble with incarnate existence is that EVERYONE FORGETS WHAT THEY ESSENTIALLY ALREADY KNOW ... that everything is merely Joy. This causes no small amount of Pure Goofiness in terms of human behaviors that manifest as greed, lust, manipulation, etc.

There is no need for any of these things, as the individual is *already blissfully happy and complete at a certain level of consciousness.* The process of Spiritual Growth is merely the simple unfoldment of the awareness that this is the case. In the Dancing Ocean of Consciousness, there are many individualized expressions of Pure Consciousness, and these are going about activities which are guaranteed to bring them to a good and wonderful place, eventually.

This is apparent to only a very few incarnate individuals, as most everyone else regards the physical realm as the only one in which "living" goes on, so let's get it while we can!! It is not until the individualized condensation of Pure Consciousness realizes that their birthright is Life and this simple thing cannot be taken away, that they are capable of moving into a place where they view any Realm of existence as a place of experience and then learn to merely OBSERVE THE DANCE OF CONSCIOUSNESS.

Bliss Is Everywhere Now

"All paths eventually resolve
in Wholeness-Being."
Steven Ridley

So where does this all bring us? It possibly brings us to a very interesting place where, instead of constant struggle, strife and battle to "get ahead," all we really have to learn is how to **relax** into the Joy, Bliss and Freedom that is ours *right now* and cannot be taken away. This is the Ancient Wisdom which is also ever new and wide as the sky. Through the utilization of one or more of the wonderful disciplines that refine the cerebrospinal system, each individual human can unfold various aspects of their Innate or Original Nature. This usually takes some small amount of time and faithful, daily practice of whichever discipline or disciplines the individual engages in, but the payoff in the end is greater than the individual can initially possibly imagine. From my experience, I would merely say this: start spiritual practice and start today!

Immersed in an Infinite Sea of Joy, we can connect with the Bliss that lies at the core of our Being at **all** times. In every moment and through every experience Bliss and Love dwell constantly in our innermost Being. It is merely over-involvement with the mental, emotional, and physical bodies, coupled with pervasive focus on happenings in the Physical Plane, that keeps us from the Innate experience of "Blissful relaxed Beingness" right now. In fact, as the channeled information suggests time and time again, *simple relaxation is the key* to accessing the higher states of experiential consciousness. It's easy ... just relax and enjoy, enjoy, enjoy!

The period of planetary history that we are passing through is a very interesting one ... a time of expansion of consciousness and evolution of the human species into something, well, MORE! This period will not be without growth pangs of various sorts, but the old way of human interaction based in power and fear is being superseded by one centered in love. As change is often disturbing to humans, many will resist this initially, but merely "going with the flow" is always the way of greatest happiness and satisfaction. What can there be to fear in an Infinite Ocean of Bliss?

In every fiber of your Being you are vibrantly alive NOW!! Don't wait around for some other day ... **Bliss Is Everywhere Now!** You are a powerful spiritual being out looking for expression and a Good Time. To access this Bliss at a greater level may require some simple daily spiritual practice over a period of time because that is the way of the physical reality ... things take time to manifest and must be worked on, whether it is losing weight or gaining experiential results from spiritual practice. But the "work" is nothing compared to the results ... you will find yourself on an adventure that you will be profoundly grateful for if you take the ride.

In the end, there is not much to say about Bliss, or any of the spiritual experiences, for they must be **experienced** and no amount of potent and flowery language can describe them adequately. I might tell you that one type of Bliss experience is like the intensity of really good sexual climax ... merely more continuous ... and this would be a good "limited" description but would still not capture the wide variety of Bliss/Joy experiences. It's the great mystic secret of the ages, but don't believe me, find out for yourself by spiritual practice.

The refinement of the cerebrospinal system is the "built-in" divine evolutionary mechanism in man. This process merely allows greater and greater access to the permanent state of consciousness possessed by the individual. As this process occurs, Innate Qualities naturally unfold, including that ol' cosmic glue that holds it all together ... LOVE. Love can be best thought of as an energy and not an emotion, although there are, of course, emotional components that accompany it while one is present in the Physical and Astral realms.

The yogis of India proclaim that each human fundamentally can be found eager to realize three things: Existence, Consciousness, and Bliss. The Dalai Lama and other avatars and followers of Buddha Shakyamuni say that it is natural for humans to attempt to seek happiness and avoid suffering. I propose that if one will just **relax into Joy**, happiness, and eventually everything else, takes care of itself. Through the long Chain of Lives of reincarnation, the individualized essence of Pure Consciousness learns, gradually, to go toward what it is drawn to and to *love everything now*. It's a simple lesson, really; it's merely that we complicate it so.

The Physical Plane is a playground of experience for consciousness units and the Essential Nature of no one is harmed by any of these experiences. The process of spiritual growth is one of unfoldment and remembrance and occurs gradually through the natural process of reincarnation or much more rapidly through the natural process of chi/prana utilization and accumulation, which can be accessed through many different disciplines and practices. There is no "One True Way" but instead **many different ways** that lead to the same place of Unity consciousness or Realization.

There is no enemy. Or maybe, there is no enemy save one: fear. Fear is an element and factor of the lower mind, which incorrectly perceives the nature of reality to be about separation, struggle, competition and lack. But there is no lack and perfection is everywhere. In this Ocean of Consciousness, Joy is all there is anywhere.

Bibliography

Bentov, Itzhak. ***Stalking the Wild Pendulum.*** Destiny Books, Rochester, VT, 1977.

Carey, Ken. ***The Starseed Transmissions.*** Harper San Francisco, San Francisco, CA, 1991.

Christensen, Alice. ***The American Yoga Association Beginner's Manual.*** Simon and Schuster, NY, NY, 1987.

Davis, Roy Eugene. ***Creative Imagination.*** CSA Press, Lakemont, GA, 1988.

Davis, Roy Eugene. ***Life Surrendered In God.*** CSA Press, Lakemont, GA, 1995.

Patten, Leslie. ***Biocircuits.*** H. J. Kramer Inc., Tiburon, CA, 1988.

Raphaell, Katrina. ***Crystal Enlightenment.*** Aurora Press, Santa Fe, NM, 1985.

Ridley, Steven. ***Breathing Methods for Health and Harmony.*** Whale Productions, 1921 Jasmine St., Denver, CO, 80220, 1992. Contact Steven at this address to procure this very useful book.

Ridley, Steven. ***Perspectives in Motion and Stillness.*** Good Karma Publishing, Fort Yates, ND, 1989.

Roeder, Dorothy. ***Crystal Co-Creators.*** Light Technology Pub., Sedona, AZ, 1994.

Scallion, Gordon-Michael. ***Notes from the Cosmos.*** Matrix Institute, Chesterfield, NH, 1997.

Selby, John. ***Kundalini Awakening.*** Bantam Books, New York, NY, 1992.

Silbey, Uma. ***The Complete Crystal Guidebook.*** Bantam Books, New York, NY, 1987.

Stone, Justin. ***Meditation for Healing.*** Good Karma Publishing, Inc., Fort Yates, ND, 1993.

Vande Kieft, Kathleen. ***Innersource: Channeling Your Unlimited Self.*** Ballantine Books, New York, NY, 1988.

Yogananda, Paramahansa. ***Autobiography of a Yogi.*** Self-Realization Fellowship, Los Angeles, CA, 1946.

Yukteswar, Swami Sri. ***The Holy Science.*** Self-Realization Fellowship, Los Angeles, CA, 1949.

Index

Absolute, 24, 104, 110, 114
  discussion of, 105-106
abundance, 9, 34-35, 59, 138
Antahkarana, 59-60, 65
Astral Plane, 86, **87-88**, 133, 142

biocircuits, 83
Bliss
  description of, 22, 142
  technique, 77
Buddhism, 21, 27, 42-44, 46, 59, 60, 69, 73-75, 101, 105, 118, 142

Causal Realities, 86, **90-91**, 102
cerebrospinal refinement, 2, 6, 27, 32, 33, 37, 51-54, 63, 65, 66, 84, 87, 89, 97, 127, 134, 141
  discussion of, 39-41, 128, 142
chakra, 48, 61, 67, 69, 72-75, 78, 79-82, 86, 127
  definition of, 13-14
change, 6, 24, 55, 57, 63, 81, 110, 114, 115, 120, 124-126, 129, 130-133, 135
  prediction of future, 95
channeling, "how-to," 16
chi, 13, 48, 49, 63, 65, 67-70, 83, 143
chi kung, 32, 36, 40, 68
cleansing, 26, 47, **55-56**, 61, 71, 74, 82, 95, 131
competition, 20, 24, 39, 58, 59, 111
Consciousness
  condensation of, **10**, 28, 29, 32, 62, 77, 94, 100, **102-104**, 107, **111-113**
  Pure Consciousness, **10-12**, 29, 47, 73, **97-98**, 102, 104-105, 108, **111-113**, 114, 127
  Supreme Consciousness, 3, 9, 26, 41, 128
  transcendent, 102, **105-106**, 110, 136
crystals, use of, 78-82

Devas, 88, **91-92**

Emptiness, 105
Enlightenment, 15, 30, 39, 42, 139
  discussion of, 50

fear, 13, 18, 25, 27, 30, 38, 47, 57, 62, 74, 81, 95, 98, 110, 115, 119-120, 123, **125**, 132, 141,143
  nature of, 8, 16, 101
freedom, 31-33, 47, 50-51, 54, 56, 57, 90, 102, 108, 130, 138-139, 141
  nature of, 119-120, 122

God, 3, 17, 18, 29, 42, 77, 88, 93, 97, 104, 107, 108, 111, 128
  discussion of, 105-106
Great Pyramid, 133-134
gunas, 9, 106

hologram, 29, 41, **109-110**, 112

ignorance, 20, 27, 30, 58, 116, 117, 135
Immortal, 25, 46, 54, 62, 67, **94-95**, 100, 103-105, 109, 116, 120, 130
Innate Nature, 6, 7, 37, 40, 42, 51, 54, **110**, 120
intention, 54, 64, 87, 138

Joy
  actualization of, **26-27**, 91-92

kundalini, 9, 12, 32, 65, **67-69**, 71
  definition of, 13

Leela, 115-117
life purpose, 18, 107, **113**

mantra
  use of, 72-76
meditation, 7, 14, 15, 22, 46, 50, 80, 83, 124
  discussion of, 41-42
  practice of, 75-77
Mental Plane, 86, **88-90**
Microcosmic Orbit, 69
millennial events, 3, 123, 129, 131
mind, 18, 23, 28, 30, 36, 40, 44, 53, 56, 58, 69, 81, 92, 95, 96, 103-105, 110-111, 116, 118, 136
  nature of, 8, 9, 11, 15, **16**, 45-46, 52, 64, **101**, 119
money, 21, 28, 35, 57, 109, 114, 129
  manifesting of, 137-138

Om, 9, **22**, 77, **106**
  chanting of, 73
Orgone blanket, 47-49, 83

Perfection, 8, 15, 20, 28, 33, 34, 37, 65, **99**, 109, 113, **117**, 122, 135
  maximizing knowledge of, 100-101
Physical Plane, 7, 11, 14, 16, 20, 24, 29, 31, 37, 44, 46, 52, 55, 63, 86-91, 93-95, 106, 109, 111, 114, 117, 124
  nature of, 95-96, 126, 134
potentiality, 41, 72, 105
prana, 65, 67, 70-72, 82, 84
pranayama, 51
  practice of, 70-71

Reiki, 12, 40, 43-45, 59
relaxing, 7, 8, 12, 25, 27, 30-34, 39, 41, 42, 52-55, **56-57**, 58, 60, 62, 67, 83, 92, 95, 99, **100**, 105, 109, **113**, 128, 135, 136, **137**, 141-142
  relaxing into life, 30, 138
remembrance, 21, 30, 95, 99
Rest Moment, 25, 123-124

serenity, 33, 34, 116
simplicity, 3, 8, 11-12, 21-23, 25, 30, 48, 54, 58, 63, 65, 92, 128, 129, **135**, 137
  discussion of, 106-107, 119
Soul, 1, 7, 14, 21, 35, 41, 56, 63, 86, 109, 132
  nature of, 28, **102-105**
star-being, 10, 29, 30
stillness, 7, 16-18, 24, 50, 68, 75-77, 83, 111

Great Moment of, 25, 40, 118, **123-126**, 128
struggle, 9, 19, 21, 31, 39, 58, 65, 116, 123, 127, 137
suffering, 3, 18, 21, 26-28, 42, 53, 55, 61, 69, 93, 99, 101, 113, 135, 142
nature of, 9, 116, **118-119**
survival, 24, **34-35**, 54, 58, 89, 125

T'ai Chi, 2, 7, 16, 23, 32, 36, 38, 39, 46, 51, 55, 65, 130
practice of, 67-68
taking action, seeing results, 101-102
Tao, 3, 36, 53, 97, 105, 126
thought-forms, 8, 34, 38, 56, 64, 88, 92, 115
"tips," 27-28, 100-101

Ultimate, 24, **105-106**
Unity, 3, 10-12, 23, 24, 94, 97, 124, 143

vibration, 13, 14, 21, 27, 30, 31, 42, 43, 47, 49, 58, 63, 64, 73, 77, 81, 83, 86-88, 93, 95, 97, 107, 124, 130, 134
nature of, 22, 106
visualization, 33, 54, 64, 69, 78

wholeness, 6, 23, 29, 41, 94, **96**, 102, 110, 112, 137
Great Wholeness, 6, 92, 97, **99**, **117**, **121**, 137
worry, 7, 8, 15, 21, **33-34**, 53, 56, 57, 89, 112, 118, **119**

For more copies of this book, contact:

Freedom Press
98 Holli Loop
Edgewood, NM 87015

Please enclose $11.95 plus $2.00 shipping and handling.